D0583249

The Jewish Holy Days
in Chasidic Philosophy

The Jewish Holy Days
in Chasidic Philosophy

NOSON GURARY

compiled and edited by
Binyomin Kaplan

JASON ARONSON INC.
Northvale, New Jersey
Jerusalem

This book was set in 11 pt. Fairfield by Alpha Graphics of Pittsfield, NH, and printed and bound by Book-Mart Press, Inc. of North Bergen, NJ.

Copyright © 2000 by Noson Gurary

10   9   8   7   6   5   4   3   2   1

All rights reserved. No part of this book may be used or reproduced in any manner whatsoever without written permission from Jason Aronson Inc. except in the case of brief quotations in reviews for inclusion in a magazine, newspaper, or broadcast.

Library of Congress Cataloging-in-Publication Data

Gurary, Natan (Guraryeh)
    The Jewish holy days in Chasidic philosophy / by Noson Gurary.
        p. cm.
    Includes bibliographical references and index.
    ISBN 0–7657–6120–3
    1. Fasts and feasts—Judaism.   2. Hasidism—Philosophy.   I. Title.
BM690.G87 2000
296.4'3—dc21   99–041041

Printed in the United States of America on acid-free paper. For information and catalog, write to Jason Aronson Inc., 230 Livingston Street, Northvale, NJ 07647-1726, or visit our website: www.aronson.com

In loving memory of a dear soul,
Avraham Ben Shlomo Picciotto,
who passed away the twenty-seventh of Tishrei.
May his soul be bound in the life of eternity,
among the souls of the righteous.

Contents

1

ॐ

"These Are the Festivals of God . . ."

A certain teaching occupies a unique place in the development of the Chasidic movement:[1]

One particular teaching was the first that the Maggid of Mezeritch heard from the Ba'al Shem Tov, and this was the teaching through which the Maggid "took" Rabbi Schneur Zalman of Liadi (that is, this teaching inspired Rabbi Schneur Zalman to become the Maggid's student). When Rabbi Schneur Zalman of Liadi prepared his son, R. Dov Ber (the "Mittler Rebbe"), to become a Rebbe, he repeated the teaching saying, "With this teaching Grandfather [the Ba'al Shem Tov] sanctified the Maggid, and this sanctification is the concept of the giving of the Torah: This is the first teaching that I heard from my master [the Maggid]:

---

1. *Sefer Hasichot*, 2nd day of *Shavuot*, 5696; reprinted in *Keter Shem Tov*, additions, p. 148.

"Eilah mo'adei Hashem"—"These are the festivals of God"—This refers to the festivals as they exist in the spiritual dimension of Torah. "The Torah preceded the world by 2000 years" and it waited for the giving of the Torah and the Jewish people.

"mikra'ei kodesh"—"holy assemblies" ["mikra'ei" can also be translated as related to "kara"—"to invite"], meaning that the supernal holiness ["kodesh elyon"—of the holidays as they exist in the spiritual realm] must be drawn down into the physical realm.

"asher tikra'u otam bemoadam"—"which you shall proclaim at their appointed times"[2] —this elicitation is by means of the preparation before the holiday.

What was the appeal and importance of this particular teaching? In order to answer this question, we must examine it further. The phrase *mikra'ei kodesh* can also be interpreted by translating the word *mikra'ei* as "calling" and eliciting, as when one person calls (*kara*) another to come to him. In the same way we must "call" and draw down the infinite light into the physical world. And this is accomplished through the preparation before a holiday.

The statement of the Sages that "Torah preceded the world by 2000 years"[3] also requires some explanation. According to chasidic philosophy, this statement does not refer literally to 2000 years; before the world's creation there was no concept of time. Rather, the statement means that the Torah is much higher than the world, existing on a level corresponding to "2000 years." The phrase "2000 years" itself refers to the spiritual level of the attributes of *chach-*

---

2. Leviticus 23:4.
3. *Midrash Tehillim*, Psalms 90:4.

mah and *binah*, wisdom and understanding.[4] The divine attributes include intellectual and emotional ones, and the world was created through the emotional ones, as explained in the *Zohar* on the verse, "For six days God created the heavens and earth."[5] The six days themselves are the six divine attributes through which the world was created. Since creation is an ongoing process, on the first day of the week (Sunday) *chesed*—kindness—radiates etc., so that every day expresses a different divine attribute. Thus, the world is associated with the divine emotional attributes, while the Torah is associated with the loftier intellectual attributes.

The connection of the emotional attributes to the world can be explained by way of analogy by noting that in a human being the emotional attributes exist for the sake of another person. In intellectually working something out another person can be a distraction, but kindness must be kindness *to* someone. The intellectual attributes, by contrast, are naturally aloof. Thus, the saying that "the Torah preceded the world by 2000 years," which associates the Torah with God's intellectual attributes, means that the Torah is completely beyond the world.[6]

This understanding of the loftiness of Torah enables us to understand what is so significant in the Baal Shem Tov's teaching, why it "took" the Maggid and his successors. The phrase "These are the festivals of God" refers to the festivals as they exist in the

---

4. The root of the Hebrew word for thousand, *elef*, can also mean "teach." As stated in chasidic philosophy (*Likkutei Torah, Shir Hashirim* 1:4), two thousand can mean two types of teaching, as stated in the verse, "I will teach you (*a'alefcha*) wisdom, I will teach you understanding" (Job 33:33).

5. Exodus 31:17; seemingly it should read "For *on* six days," and the omission of the word "on" means that it can be read as "six days created."

6. *Sefer Hama'amarim* 5653, *Ita Bemidrash Tehillim.*

loftiest spiritual dimension of Torah. The key insight of the Baal Shem Tov's teaching, however, is that even though the Torah is much higher than the world, nevertheless the physical realm has an important advantage. The Ba'al Shem Tov explains that the Jewish people's fulfillment of the Torah in the physical world, in the realm of time and space, is such a precious thing that the Torah, "waited for the giving of the Torah and Israel" so that the holiness of the Torah in the spiritual realm could be drawn down to the physical world.

Thus, for all the loftiness of the revelations in the spiritual realm, God desired the spiritual service of human beings in the physical world. Moreover, this advantage of the lower realms is also "felt" in the spiritual realm; it is perceived there that the intention of all the divine revelations in the spiritual world is that ultimately they should be "drawn down" into the physical realm. Even though we exist in the lowest of all worlds, nevertheless it was precisely this world that God desired for a "dwelling place," a place where His essence is revealed.

The chasidic master Rabbi Avraham Yehoshua Heschel of Apt, on the verse we have been discussing, *"Eilah Mo'adei,"*[7] explains that we draw down holiness on a holiday from a level which is higher than time into time. This level is the level of divine thought on which God first has the desire to condense Himself[8] in order to create the world. Although it is higher than time, on this level there is already a desire to create time. When we cleave to God on this level we elicit God's love for the Jewish people, for whose sake the world was created.

---

7. *Oheiv Yisrael, Derushim Lepesach.*

8. This is the concept of *tzimtzum.* See the chapters on Rosh Hashanah and Shabbat for further explanation.

A holiday's commemoration of a particular event means that a certain spiritual revelation, the one associated with the original event, reoccurs on that day. We might ask "Why is it not possible to draw it down on another day?" The answer is that each day has a special quality not found in any other, for each has its own life force that is relevant to that particular time. On a holiday, the original revelation caused the life force of that day to become refined in a way that makes it a vessel for a particular "light." Therefore, it can only become manifest when the same day comes up again on the calendar.

Another concept connected to holidays is that the spiritual revelation associated with a particular holiday has an influence on the whole year, as is explained in many works of chasidic philosophy. Rosh Hashanah, for instance, sets the tone of the whole year in connection to a person's fear of heaven. Similarly, Sukkot, Shemini Atzeret, and Simchat Torah provide the joy of fulfilling a mitzvah for the whole year.[9]

Another chasidic master, Rabbi Wolf of Zhitomir, explains that each holiday represents a specific divine attribute. For instance Pesach represents *chesed*—kindness—and Shavuot represents *tiferet*—beauty. By means of this attribute a spiritual level called *tov* is revealed, which is higher than the divine attributes, and therefore holidays are called *Yamim Tovim*.[10]

Rabbi Menachem Nachum of Chernobyl also discusses each holiday as a spiritual reoccurence of the event it commemorates. For instance, on the original Pesach, the Jewish people departed from "the 49 gates of impurity."[11] Thus, every Pesach the Jewish

---

9. *Likkutei Sichot*, vol. 9, p. vii.

10. *Or Hameir al Megillat Ester*. See also *Avodat Yisrael* by the Maggid of Kosnitz, citing *Tikkunei Zohar, Tikkun 23*.

11. See chapter on Pesach.

people escape from all the *kelipot* (spiritual entities which embody evil). If not for the "Holiday of Matzot" every year, a person would not have the strength to break through the *kelipot* to strengthen his attachment to God.

Similarly, Rabbi Menachem Nachum continues, on Shavuot, everyone receives the Torah anew, determining what *seichel* (intellectual level) he will be granted to serve God that year. On Sukkot we are surrounded by the kindness of God, just as in the wilderness we were surrounded by the clouds of glory. On Purim, the time of the downfall of *Amaleik*, just as originally there was energy strong enough to destroy wickedness, every year we receive a special granting of ability to nullify spiritual impurity. In the original events of Chanukah, secularists wanted to get rid of the *chukim*, the *mitzvot* which were given simply as divine decrees unaccompanied by any explanation of their purpose. Every Chanukah we strengthen ourselves in keeping *chukim*.[12]

There is another important point in the teaching of the Ba'al Shem Tov that we have been discussing. It is not only that the advantage of the lower level is felt in the spiritual revelation of the holiday as it exists above and that this revelation is elicited in the physical world at a certain time through our spiritual service. This "drawing down" of the spiritual itself creates the "dwelling place" for God is discussed above. This means that through *mikra'ei kodesh*, drawing down the holiness of the holiday from above, we actually draw down God's essence into time and space.

According to this, another puzzling matter is also explained: How is it possible that in different places the times for reciting the *Shema* are different and that *Shabbat* and other holidays start and end at different times? It is explained by Rabbi Schneur

---

12. *Ma'or Einaim, Parshat Mikeitz.*

Zalman of Liadi[13] that spiritually these times are "above the categories of time and place. It is only that they radiate below in each place at the time which is proper for it. This is also the reason that the holiness of a holiday can be in effect outside the land of Israel on the second day of each holiday celebrated only in the Disapora. Thus, even residents of Israel who travel outside of Israel are obligated concerning the holiness of these days, even though their intent is to return back to Israel."

Besides the fact that a particular light shines every holiday, every year a higher light shines then in the past year, which means that the well-known precept[14] that one should increase in matters of holiness also exists in the spiritual realm. A second reason for this yearly increase is that the cumulative spiritual light elicited by all the *mitzvot* that the Jewish people have performed is increased by the *mitzvot* that were done in the past year. Thus, we draw down a higher light than previously. Thus, the concept of *Yom Tov* is not only to remember what happened and to learn the greatness of the Creator from it—rather, on a deeper level, the event is reoccurring now on this holiday with greater intensity than at any time during the thousands of years which have past.

The purpose of the present work is to explain the nature of the spiritual revelation associated with each holiday, and also *Shabbat*, the holy day which takes place each week. The concept of a recurring spiritual revelation illuminates the various themes and observances of each holiday, revealing the conceptual unity underlying each one and providing insight into what the individual worshipper can accomplish on each one in the service of God.

---

13. *Shulchan Aruch, Hilchot Hashkamat Haboker* 1:8.
14. *Berachot* 28a.

As we discuss each holiday, it may often seem to the reader that each one is being described as the high point of the Jewish calendar. Seemingly, they cannot all be the greatest holiday. However, this successive feeling that each holiday is the greatest of them all is wholly appropriate and one of the key insights provided by studying each one according to chasidic philosophy. Each holiday contains a special quality not contained in any of the others that provides a unique connection between the Jewish people and God.

Since each holiday embodies one of the primary themes of Jewish worship, what ultimately emerges from a consideration of all the holidays is an overview of Judaism itself. In the continuing spiritual avocation of the Jewish people, which is bringing holiness to all aspects of mundane human activity, each holiday represents a unique granting of spiritual strength from above, enabling the individual Jew to approach his spiritual mission with renewed vigor and joyousness.

2

ک

Rosh Hashanah: The Coronation of the King

"The first day of the seventh month shall be a day of rest, a holy convocation for remembrance and the sounding of the *shofar*." (Leviticus 23:24)

"And in the seventh month, on the first day of the month, you shall have a holy convocation: You shall not do any forbidden labor, it will be for you a day of the blowing of the *shofar*." (Numbers 29:1)

Rosh Hashanah is known as "the Birthday of the World," "the Day of Remembrance," and "the Day of Judgement." Although each of these three designations of Rosh Hashanah seems quite different, *Chassdut* demonstrates that every aspect of the holiday relates to a single theme.

Chasidic philosophy explains that the key spiritual event of Rosh Hashanah is the renewal of God's Kingship which we bring about through *hachtarat hamelech* (the coronation of the King). This means that we submit ourselves to God with our total being and entreat Him to reveal His Kingship "below," in the physical world. Our request that God reveal His Kingship is the constant theme of the liturgy of Rosh Hashanah since we seek to elicit God's will to reign and His delight in being King for the whole year.[1]

THE NATURE OF KINGSHIP

The Talmud states that kingship (in Hebrew, *malchut*) on earth parallels kingship in heaven.[2] An earthly king requires someone to be king over, as indicated by the saying "there is no king without a people."[3] The divine attribute of *malchut* is similarly connected to that which God creates and rules over. God's creation of the world through *malchut* is what makes possible an existence that perceives itself as being independent of God.

A king is essentially one who is exalted over his subjects and therefore removed from them. His personality is concealed from the people, and his main interaction with them is through issuing decrees. The divine attribute of *malchut* also has the quality of being exalted, and here also this exaltation can be described as concealment. God conceals His true "light"[4] so that the world perceives itself as an independent entity. If God had created the world through any other faculty than *malchut*, the world would not have a sense of autonomous existence. The world would simply appear as an extension of God's light, and Human beings would

---

1. In kabbalistic terminology *Keter Malchut*.

2. *Berachot* 58a; *Zohar* I 157a; *Zohar* III 176b.

3. *See Sha'ar Hayichud Veha'emunah*, ch. 7.

4. Light is the preferred metaphor in Jewish mysticism for divine influence and creative force.

then be unable to exercise free will to serve God by fulfilling Torah and *mitzvot*.

God, to use the chasidic terminology, desired a *dirah betachtonim*—a dwelling place in the lower realms, the mundane physical world. Chasidic philosophy frequently explains that the spiritual realm consists of a succession of "worlds" or levels in which the revelation of Godliness is progressively diminished and the feeling of self becomes more prevelant among the entities that exist on each level. Each level possesses an attribute of *malchut*, which is the link that enables the next lower level to come into being from it. *Malchut* accomplishes this by concealing the higher level so that the lower one can exist. It operates, thus, on every spiritual level. The intent is finally the lowest level, this lowly physical world in which Divinity is so hidden that it is even possible for created beings to think that they exist independently of God. It is nevertheless God's will, the ultimate purpose of creation, that we should transform this world into a divine dwelling, a place where Godlines is revealed. Since kingship is the faculty that enables "the lower realms" to come into existence at all, it obviously plays a crucial role.

On Rosh Hashanah we are particularly concerned that God's creation of the world should be with pleasure since something done with enthusiasm cannot be compared to something done merely perfunctorily, as will be explained later. We can understand this with the analogy of a learned and pious human king, who has to neglect his personal interests (his intellectual and spiritual pursuits) in order to deal with mundane matters of the country. The only way such a person is persuaded to accept kingship, a complete commitment to his subjects' well-being, is through the outcry of the people begging him from the depths of their hearts to be king over them. Similarly, each year we must evoke God's pleasure in kingship through intense supplication and sincere entreaty. When we do so, He accepts kingship again for another year.

Malchut, unlike the other divine attributes, can only be elicited when certain conditions are met. The reason is that *malchut*, unlike the other *middot*, is rooted in the essence of the soul and its nature is to be aloof and exalted. As Chasidic philosophy frequently explains, the emotions and intellectual attributes are not the soul itself, which is essentially simplistic. The essence of the soul is totally removed from any of the soul's attributes, and this is the source of the exaltedness of *malchut*.

Just as the human attribute of kingship is rooted in the essence of the soul, the divine attribute of *malchut* is rooted in God's essence.[5] Since the nature of essence is to be remote and totally removed from anything else, the natural tendency of *malchut* is to remain in its source and not become revealed. Therefore, the Jewish people must exert tremendous effort on Rosh Hashanah to affect God's essence, evoking a delight in reigning.[6]

---

5. More specifically, *malchut* is rooted in the level called *reisha dela ityada*—the head which is not known. Kabbalistic sources also use the phrasing *dela yada vela ityada*—which does not know and which is not known—implying that it is not known even to itself. (See references in *Sefer Hama'amarim Melukat*, vol. 2, p.107.)

6. The fact that *malchut* is rooted in the essence of the soul leads to a difference between how *malchut* and the other attributes are expressed. The attributes of the soul must evolve through a series of stages. There is the level on which there is the potential for the revelation of the soul and then a level on which this revelation actually takes place, enabling the soul to relate to something outside of itself through different emotions.

On the level where there is a potential for revelation, *malchut*, unlike the other attributes, is in a state known in Chasidic philosophy as *helem she'eino bemetziut*—concealment without existence—and *helem she'eino shayich legilui*—concealment which is beyond becoming revealed. (An

We can understand this by considering the attribute of kingship in a human being. Every person possesses ten faculties corresponding to God's ten attributes, three intellectual faculties of *chachmah* (wisdom), *binah* (understanding), and *da'at* (knowledge), and seven emotional ones, ending with *malchut* (kingship).

All nine attributes, aside from *malchut*, are self-directed. Intellect seeks to acquire knowledge that will benefit the person, for instance. The six emotional attributes, excluding *malchut*, are orientated toward loving what is beneficial for the person and disliking what is harmful to him. Since these emotions are self-directed, they exist even when they are not openly revealed, and therefore a person can be in a desolate wilderness and actively express all nine faculties.

We see this, for example, in Abraham's desire for guests. The beginning of *parshat Vayeira*[7] indicates that he had an arousal in the feeling of kindness when there was no one around to benefit from it. In fact, he felt such an arousal of kindness that the absence of guests caused him pain. Kindness and mercy are also relevant to animals, and even to inanimate objects, as when the Talmud says that "a person has pity on his handiwork," etc.[8]

The evocation of *malchut*, in contrast, specifically requires the effort of another person. The reason is that *malchut* is essentially altruistic; true kingship exists totally for the sake of the subjects and it is of no benefit to the sovereign.[9]

---

analogy for this is the difference between fire as it exists in a burning coal and as it exists in a flint stone. In the coal the fire is currently in existence, while in a flint stone it is not only hidden, but not in existence at all.) The exalted nature of *malchut* thus makes it very hard to evoke.

7. Genesis 18:1–2, Rashi.

8. *Sefer Hama'amarim* 5688, *Tikku*.

9. This explains why we say that every person has an attribute of kingship although very few people ever achieve actual kingship. This attribute

Besides the requirement that *malchut* must be evoked by someone else besides the king, there is also the requirement that the one doing the evoking must be comparable in some sense to the king. Thus, a human king can only reign over other human beings and not animals.

A third requirement is that there must nevertheless be a certain distance between the sovereign and his subjects. The other emotions, love for instance, involve closeness between the person feeling the emotion and its object. The king's children can never simply be his subjects because the strength of the father-child bond inevitably interferes with the king-subject relationship. Due to the distance associated with *malchut,* even when the other conditions are met, the subjects must still earnestly entreat the king to rule over them and accept his kingship unquestioningly.

If we apply the foregoing analysis to God's kingship over human beings, however, conceptual difficulties arise. On one hand, if the subjects must be on the same level as the sovereign in some sense, then how can God be king over human beings, who are infinitely more distant from God's level of existence than animals are from human beings? On the other hand, the Jewish people are called "children" to God and the whole existence of every created being is unified with God since its whole existence is the power of God creating it at every moment. Therefore the whole concept of *malchut* seems to be invalidated when applied to God. How ultimately, do we elicit God's desire to accept us as His servants once again, to be King over the Universe, and to take an inner delight and pleasure in our service? The answer is that it is necessary to elicit God's choice, since choice is essentially be-

---

is expressed when a person's innermost essence is revealed in a way that is completely for the benefit of someone else.

yond reason, as explained later. God's choice derives from His essence, and the elicitation of His choice is the central theme of Rosh Hashanah as well as the purpose of sounding the *shofar*, the only mitzvah unique to the holiday.

The analogy between man's attribute of *malchut* and God's employs speech as a metaphor, analogous to the fact that an earthly king literally rules through speech, issuing decrees etc. We have also been discussing *malchut* as the medium through which God carries out creation, which is described in the Torah[10] as involving ten divine "utterances": "Let there be light" etc.

A human remains "within himself" when he merely thinks or feels; nothing becomes known to others. However, through speech, he projects "out of himself" to relate to others. As far as the speaker is concerned, the words conceal the thought more than they reveal it since it is difficult to capture a thought completely in words. To the listener, however, the words are a revelation, since otherwise he has no access to the speaker's thoughts. The speaker, in other words, limits his thought in order that it can be revealed to the listener. Similarly, God's creation of the world involves simultaneous concealment and revelation.

The comparison to speech is also another way of understanding the loftiness of the attribute of *malchut* in its source. When a person puts an idea into words, besides communicating to another person and revealing his thought, he also achieves a better understanding of the thought through articulating it. This indicates that the source of speech, like *malchut*, is the innermost essence of the soul, higher than intellect and emotions, and this leads to another important point.

---

10. *Pirkei Avot* 5:1.

BEYOND WORDS

The Ba'al Shem Tov explains that according to its inner meaning, the sound of the *shofar* is not only wordless, but beyond words. On Rosh Hashanah we must evoke God's delight in creating the world through *malchut* (or words), and therefore our effort cannot simply be verbal—for we have to create a will to create the world through words, and will is higher than speech. We have to reach the source of divine speech, God's essence, through the inner voice that stems from our essence.

Why is this particularly through a sound? The answer lies in the fact that all spiritual revelations from one level to another require an intermediary that combines aspects of both levels. Otherwise the higher level is so totally beyond the lower one that it has no basis for influencing it.[11] Whenever one uses the voice, at least one letter is always sounded, since the speech organs have to be in some configuration. This letter is an intermediate stage between mere undifferentiated sound and full-fledged speech. This is the sound emitted when a person expresses himself from the depths of his heart in a simple wordless cry, an expression of a level deeper than speech can express. When we want to awaken God's delight to create the world with *malchut*—words—it has to come from our awakening our delight in a form without letters. In other words, we have to express a level within ourselves that is deeper than words to evoke a level in God that is "deeper than words" and which thus can serve as their source.

---

11. *Seder Tefillot Mikol Hashanah, Sha'ar Hatekiot*, 244b.

THE WITHDRAWAL OF KINGSHIP

Since every holiday is a spiritual reoccurrence of the events commemorated, and Rosh Hashanah is the "Birthday of the World" as we will explain, before every Rosh Hashanah the spiritual state that existed prior to creation reoccurs. Therefore, before Rosh Hashanah God's will to reign and His delight in reigning withdraw. The "external dimension of *malchut*," God's minimal effort to keep the world in existence, remains only because of God's covenant with Noah never again to destroy the world.

When Adam was created on Rosh Hashanah, he immediately accepted God's Kingship. He cried out that all creation should accept God's Kingship, and God's purpose for creating the world was immediately realized. Thus, we also need to arouse God's delight in creation from His essence, as Adam did. This is done through *haktarat hamelech* with the acceptance of the yoke of His kingdom, and most essentially by blowing the *shofar*.

Another reason for the withdrawal of the previous year's choice by God to take pleasure in being King over the Jewish nation, the essence of *malchut*, is that it was accepted in the first place for one year. The result is far-reaching: the world exists as if God no longer takes pleasure in creating it. Until the blowing of the *shofar* it is as if the world is fainting. God's work in maintaining creation is analogous then to labor done by a tired person who takes no pleasure in his work.

For instance, one might imagine a builder who once had some grandiose plan but who loses his enthusiasm in the middle of the project. Consequently, he does the job superficially, and his work is perfunctory throughout the remainder of the construction. In the same way, since God's delight in reigning withdraws on the eve of Rosh Hashanah, the world only continues to exist superficially.

Another way to understand the spiritual withdrawal before Rosh Hashanah is by way of analogy. A father who wants to understand his son's wisdom hides from him to see if the son will realize that his father is not truly absent, but only testing to see if his son will search for him. In addition to searching, a wise son also demonstrates his wisdom in the methods he uses to search. Thus, the father rejoices in his son's wisdom demonstrated by his understanding, and his son's love, demonstrated by the intensity of the pursuit. Ultimately, the father and son's joy in being reunited is greater than the joy of uninterrupted togetherness.

Similarly, the spiritual withdrawal of Rosh Hashanah is not true concealment of Godliness, but only so that the Jewish people will entreat God from the depths of their hearts to accept Kingship. The ultimate result is the rejoicing revealed on Sukkot. And this is what is meant by the verse "Blow the *shofar* on the new moon, at the appointed time of our holiday."[12] The Hebrew for "on the appointed day of our holiday" (*bakesseh leyom chageinu*) can be translated as "hidden for the day of our holiday." Thus, the ultimate intention of the concealment on the eve of Rosh Hashanah is the revelation of joy "on the day of our holiday," Sukkot, which is known as "the time of our rejoicing."

The withdrawal on Rosh Hashanah also occurs because the new divine light that will shine into the world is loftier than the light of all the years before.[13] The reason for this is two-fold: the merits of the Jewish people have reached a new level through the merits accumulated during the year, and also God fulfills the same

---

12. Psalms 81:4.
13. *Igeret Hakodesh*, ch. 14.

commandments that He gives to us. Thus, just as He constantly commands us to add to our merits, He adds new energy to the world every year that it has never experienced before.

Since God desires all spiritual "energies" to be bestowed as a result of man's spiritual service, we must exert more effort than in the previous year to restore God's pleasure in creation and draw down the new supernal light.[14] The Ba'al Shem Tov explains that in the phrase *Tiku bachodesh shofar* (Blow the *shofar* on the New Moon)[15]—the word *chodesh* is related to *chidush* (something new). This refers to a renewal that we achieve on the highest level of our faculty of delight.[16] Rabbi Schneur Zalman of Liadi also explains that the word *shofar*, aside from meaning "horn," is also related to the word for *delight*,[17] which is the theme of Rosh Hashanah, as we have been saying. Our evocation within God of a new delight in kingship is accomplished by our creating a new, hitherto unachieved delight in ourselves.

THE BIRTHDAY OF THE WORLD

The concept of Rosh Hashanah as "birthday of the world" is also found in the liturgy of Rosh Hashanah in the statement, "This is

---

14. The removal of God's will and His pleasure is not only in the physical world but also in all the spiritual worlds, for every level is insignificant compared to God and stands to remain insignificant unless God accepts kingship once again.

15. Psalms 81:4.

16. In kabbalistic terminology *penimiut hata'anug*, the "inner dimension of delight." Also, our service to God is with our inner delight (see *Keter Shem Tov*, sec. 119 and 256).

17. *Likkutei Torah, Derushim Lerosh Hashanah* 54c.

the day, the beginning of Your works."[18] Chasidic philosophy asks, how it can be called the "beginning of Your works" when the world was created five days earlier? Rosh Hashanah is actually celebrated on the sixth day of creation, when man was created, the last of all creations. The answer is that God's desire for a "dwelling in the lower realms" can only be fulfilled through man's efforts to elevate the world to be a vessel for God's presence. Thus, Adam, and man in general, is the center and purpose for the whole creation and the "beginning of Your works" is the sixth day.

We can explore this further. The celebration of the "birthday of the world" does not focus on Adam's body, but on his unique soul. Adam's body, as the Torah states, was taken from the earth, which was created on the first day. It is the creation of man's soul, which God "blew" into Adam's body, that we celebrate on Rosh Hashanah.

The scriptural statement about man's soul being blown indicates a difference between man and all other created beings, whose bodies and souls were made from God's utterances, as explained above. As the *Zohar* explains,[19] "one who blows, blows from within." This indicates that the source of the soul is the innermost aspect of God. Rabbi Schneur Zalman of Liadi, in the Tanya, adds an additional insight to the statement of the *Zohar*. Not only is blowing "from within," but "with strength,"[20] unlike normal speech, which does not require strength. Spiritually, this means that a force which is greater than the soul is required to unite the

---

18. Liturgy, *Musaf Amidah* for Rosh Hashanah; discussed in *Rosh Hashanah* 27a.

19. This is the attribution given in *Tanya*, ch. 2 based, evidently, on a version of the text that differs from current printed editions.

20. *Igeret Hateshuvah*, ch. 4, 94a.

opposites of the supremely lofty soul and the lowly body. This means that man not only lives from his soul, but from the essence of God joining the soul and body together. Since man has a special connection to God's essence, he is able to elicit it.[21]

A question arises from the Talmud's statement that the world was created on *chaf-hey* Elul, the twenty fifth of Elul. What does this mean in reference to the original creation, if time had not yet been created? Chasidic philosophy explains that the world was originally created with the spiritual light of *chaf-hey* Elul. This can be explained in two ways:

Every day possesses its own unique divine "light" that gives it a different spiritual character than every other day of the year. According to this, the creation of the world on *chaf-hey* Elul refers to the particular lofty quality of the light used.

Another explanation is that each day of the year possesses the accumulated light of all the days that preceded it, so that each day of the year has a greater light than that which has shone during the year previously. Therefore, the statement that the world was created on *chaf-hey Elul* means that the "quantity" of light used was the same as that accumulated for eleven months and twenty-five days.

There is a deeper dimension, however, to the phrase *chaf-hey* Elul. The two letters *chaf-hey* also spell the Hebrew word *koh*, meaning "so" or "like this." In the above-discussed phrase, "This is the day, the beginning of Your works," the word translated as "this" is *zeh*. The difference between *koh* and *zeh* is discussed in

---

21. The source of the soul in the body (as "blown" into the body) is from the inner aspect of God's pleasure, in mystical terminology *bechinat penimiut hata'anug*, which is a means for ultimately reaching the inner dimension of God's essence, *bechinat penimiut ha'atzmut* and therefore only a soul in a body can cause a divine response from this level.

the Midrash,[22] which states that, unlike Moses, all the other prophets used the term *koh* (like this) in the phrase, "Thus spoke God." The other prophets did not experience the revelation of God's essence, but only glimmers of divine revelation apprehended through visions. Moses, in contrast, prophesied using the word *zeh* in the phrase "this is what God said" (i.e. "this is exactly what God said"). Thus, only Moses experienced a revelation of God's essence, which is the only true referent of the word *zeh* (this).

Just as one might point to something, the thing itself, and say "this is it,"[23] *zeh* in reference to God refers to His essence. Thus, since God is the only true independent existence and everything else depends on Him, He is the only entity that can truly be called *zeh* since something dependent on something else is essentially non-existent.

This difference involves the distinction between finitude and infinity. It is not possible to experience God's essence through finite revelation. Moses' revelation, however, was infinite and he was thus able to apprehend God's essence. Similarly, man's contribution to the world is to transform a world of *koh* to a world of *zeh*, to reveal God's essence. This is the same idea as eliciting God's kingship over the universe. God's kingship is rooted in His essence, which is why, as discussed earlier, Adam's first action upon being created, fulfilling his purpose immediately, was to proclaim God King.

Rabbi Schneur Zalman of Liadi offers a novel explanation of the statement, "Today is the day, the beginning of Your works."

---

22. *Sifri Mattot* 2.

23. Using the analogy of light from a luminary, one would never point to the light and say "this is it," the thing itself, for the light is simply a revelation of the luminary and has no existence beyond that of the luminary. It would only make sense to say "this is it" of the luminary itself.

According to the idea that we have been discussing that God renews everything with a new light on Rosh Hashanah, one loftier than any given in past years, we are not just celebrating a "Birthday of the World" that occurred in the past. *Ze hayom techilat ma'asecha* does not mean "Today is the day that *was* originally the beginning of Your works," but, "Today *is* the day, the beginning of Your works."[24]

THE SERVICE OF A SERVANT

"The crowning of the King," the acceptance of the yoke of His kingship in the inner essence of the Jewish soul, requires the service of a true servant with devotion and dedication. A true servant devotes his entire essence to the master so that the master's yoke is constantly upon him. This is true not only when he performs his duties, but even when he eats and sleeps, and certainly it is not necessary to motivate the servant to do his work.

Unlike the acceptance of the yoke of Rosh Hashanah, the acceptance of the yoke during the year is primarily relevant to action. A person undertakes to do whatever is needed to fulfill God's will and therefore he does the *mitzvot* even if his mind and heart do not totally assent—his inner subservience to God remains hidden in his soul. During the year God's kingship is already established, but on Rosh Hashanah it is elicited anew. Therefore, the service of Rosh Hashanah requires a revelation of total subservience and submission. During the year a person's acceptance of the yoke stems from a level that is lower than intellect: simple submission. On Rosh Hashanah acceptance of the yoke is com-

---

24. *Likkutei Torah, Nitzavim* 47c.

pletely beyond intellect (and the other faculties of the soul). During the year acceptance of the yoke is the foundation of a person's performance of *mitzvot*, but on Rosh Hashanah it is the whole structure, so to speak, of the spiritual service of the day.

Since the service of Rosh Hashanah is that of a servant, we avoid sleeping as much as possible, abstain from eating excessively, and use every free moment to recite Psalms rather than delving into the Torah intellectually.[25] This accords with the well-known distinction between the king's ministers and his household servants: A minister's whole concern is with intellectual matters, and the servant's main service is with simple service, acceptance of the yoke. Since everyone is equal in this kind of service, our main activity is reciting Psalms, in which the emphasis is on simply reciting the words, thus underscoring that we are all equally servants of God.

The prayer of Rosh Hashanah night is with supplication and weeping from the depths of the heart. We entreat God to accept us as servants who serve Him by fulfilling Torah and *mitzvot*, and this is the distinctive acceptance of the yoke of Rosh Hashanah, which requires the stirring of a person's whole essence.

The focus of Rosh Hashanah, as we have been saying, is to reestablish our link with God so that the essence of God Himself should take pleasure in our service to Him, so that we become significant enough to evoke His desire to accept Kingship once again. Thus, the prayers on Rosh Hashanah, rather than stressing repentance as one might expect on the "Day of Judgement," contain the repeated reference to God as King of the Universe, for that is the theme of the day.

---

25. In fact, the service of the whole Ten Days of Repentance, including both Rosh Hashanah and Yom Kippur, must be that of a servant.

The answer to the famous question of why we don't confess and ask for forgiveness on "the day of judgement" is that first we must establish our intimate relationship with God. In fact, this is the whole purpose of Torah and *mitzvot*: To reveal the inner connection that distinguishes the Jewish people from all other created entities, who possess mere existence. Only afterwards can we be concerned with our transgressions. However, if there is a refusal of kingship, we will have no intimate relationship with God upon which to base our request for forgiveness. This intimate relationship is the inner dimension of the life force of the world, and the whole theme of Rosh Hashanah is to renew this level.

THE DAY OF JUDGEMENT

The connection between the coronation of the king and the day of judgement is that when God's delight and pleasure from the last year are removed, He views things differently, with detachment. Analogously, a detached mood in a person can be accompanied by a certain uneasiness, so that he is more sensitive to defects in the actions of others.

The connection between the coronation and the Day of Judgement can also be understood using the analogy of an earthly king. The existence of the kingdom is only for the benefit of its inhabitants, and its foundation is awe of the king and his decrees. If there were no fear or awe of the king deterring wrongdoing, there would be chaos. Similarly, in kingship in heaven, the essential idea of kingship is the maintenance of order and justice in the world, and God rewards and punishes based on what a person deserves.

In an orderly system of justice there is a prosecutor who brings evidence against the person being judged. The king listens to the prosecutor, and based on his findings, he gives a verdict. If no one demands just rulings, then justice is not carried out.

However, when we speak about God, there is no need for a prosecutor to inform God about actions that may require punishment, since God knows everything that happens. Nevertheless, in the divine system of justice, as in an earthly one, there is no passing of judgement without claims from prosecutors. The "prosecutors" in the Heavenly Court are angels who are created as a result of a person's sins.

An earthly prosecutor cannot ply his trade at all times. There is a certain time set aside when the king sits on this throne, wearing his crown of kingship, as the ruler of his domain. At that time, when the king has put on, so to speak, his awe-inspiring majesty, all claimants can come before him. However, when the king is otherwise occupied and his attention is directed to family matters, or administrative matters, or his studies, the king cannot be disturbed. The king cannot be approached when he is in a mood of kindness and mercy, and especially at a time that he is rejoicing over good news.

For God, *Shabbat* and *Yom Tov* are times of delight and then there is no judgement, just as a father is not interested in hearing complaints when he is playing with his beloved child.

Thus, for an earthly king, there is one day in particular, the anniversary of the king's coronation, the day when He again wears his crown. That is the special day of the year for all to seek justice, and each case can be brought before Him to decide a verdict so that justice can be maintained throughout the country.

Similarly, on Rosh Hashanah, God sits on His throne with his crown of kingship, which is the day that He accepts to become king once again. Like the earthly king, whose function is to maintain order, God is referred to in prayer as the "King of Justice." God listens then because the coronation of the King is directly related to maintaining order in the world.[26] The judgement itself is an allotment of each person's basic needs for the year following Rosh Hashanah, which he earns through his spiritual service throughout the year before Rosh Hashanah.

This allotment of needs for the whole year is why Rosh Hashanah is called the "head of the year," rather than the beginning of the year. The head contains the brain, which controls and influences every part of the body and which is the life force of the body as a whole.

Similarly, on Rosh Hashanah God grants an allotment, which encompasses everything that will be given to every individual on each day of the year, in spiritual matters and physical matters. No more, no less is allocated throughout the year, just as the brain includes all the forces that are on every level of the body. This is why we follow many customs that indicate that Rosh Hashanah sets the tone for the whole year, eating a fish head, eating sweet foods, not sleeping on Rosh Hashanah during the day, etc.

Why then, we might ask, do we pray three times daily during the year, asking God for all our needs, when it was all determined and allocated by God on Rosh Hashanah? A related question arises from the Talmud's statement that man is judged every day. Chasidic philosophy answers that the allocation given on Rosh Hashanah is a very general one[27] and the particulars are determined based on the judgement of man's conduct during the year. We are asking God that the general allocation should materialize in the material world in the most desirable way. It is possible that our allocation given on Rosh Hashanah can remain on a spiritual

---

26. The foregoing section is based on *Torat Chayim, Parshat Vayeira* 190ff.

27. *Likkutei Torah, Derushim Lerosh Hashanah*, 58a.

level that will only benefit our souls. Even if it does materialize, it can come to us with difficulty or pain. Our allotment may also not include what is needed for all of the three standard needs, "children, health, and livelihood," so we are concerned that whatever need is most pressing should be fulfilled.

MALCHIOT, ZICHRONOT, AND SHOFROT

Besides the biblical requirement on Rosh Hashanah to blow *shofar*, the Talmud states that the prayers are to include *malchiot*, ten verses referring to God as king of the world over the universe, *zichronot*, ten verses relating how God remembers His covenant and the merits of the Jewish people, and *shofrot*, ten verses mentioning *shofar*.

The Talmud states, "God asks us on Rosh Hashanah, 'Say verses of kingship before Me so that I should be King over you; say remembrances before Me so that your remembrances should come up to Me for good.' How does all this take place? Through *shofar*."[28]

Chasidic philosophy explains that the purpose of reciting scriptural verses is that the Torah comprises the blueprints for the world. This actually has two aspects: The Torah is the source of all creation,[29] and also the channel for all divine influence since each of the twenty-two letters of the Hebrew alphabet represents a different divine creative force. Moreover, the recitation of these

---

28. *Rosh Hashanah* 16a.

29. We also recite the three sets of ten verses because we want to create the whole structure of the attribute of kingship composed of ten faculties. This is known as *binyan hamalchut*.

verses demonstrates that our requests are based on the Torah, the absolute truth.

Our recitation of *malchiot* can also be seen as praising kingship in order to arouse God's desire for it. Chasidic philosophy gives the analogy of showing a beautiful picture to a great king. Ordinarily, the king's concerns are too exalted for him to involve himself with something so trivial. However, when his servants praise the picture and point out its beauty, the king may turn his attention from his usual lofty concerns and look at it. Once he has removed his attention from his prior concerns and once he has become somewhat interested in the picture, he actually ends up taking pleasure from it with his whole essence. Since the picture has no relevance to the king's intellect or emotions (i.e., anything external to his essence), the king actually takes pleasure from the picture on the highest level of his personality.

Similarly, the Jewish people try to arouse God's desire to take pleasure in the subservience of created beings, in the fact that even though they perceive themselves to be independent existences, they devote their whole existences to serving Him. Although God is exalted beyond being a King over human beings, their recitation of the verses of Kingship causes Him to lower Himself from the pleasure that He takes in the highest levels of His essence. In addition, as mentioned above, the recitation of verses is analogous to citing prooftexts for a particular point. It is as if we are saying to God that Kingship is pleasant and desirable, "as it is written in Your Torah," bringing scriptural support for our statement. Through this praise, He is drawn somewhat to Kingship, and then, as explained above, His whole essence is finally elicited.[30]

---

30. *Sefer Ham'amarim* 5688, pp. 16–17.

The group of verses called *zichronot* raises the question of what it means to ask that God should remember. The verses mention God's remembering His covenant with Noah, His covenants with the Patriarchs, the binding of Isaac, etc. Do we really need to remind God to remember, when to God, "there is no forgetting"? In the same *berachah* in which we ask God to remember we state, *ain shichcha lifnei kisie kevodecha*. This question is underscored by the name "The Day of Remembrance"—*Yom Hazikaron*. Even in the Torah reading on Rosh Hashanah, we read the story of how God "remembered" Sarah's prayers for a child on Rosh Hashanah. And in the same way, the *haftorah* is about Hannah and how God remembered and granted her prayers for a child, also on Rosh Hashanah.

Chasidic philosophy explains that God is exalted and infinite, and everything is insignificant compared to Him. Thus, this remembrance that we request is His choice that we should have significance. The connection between remembering and significance can be illustrated by the case of a person who sins inadvertently and is required to bring a sin-offering. An example would be a person who forgets that it is *Shabbat* and who performs one of the forbidden labors. We might ask, "Why is he punished if he merely forgot?" The answer is that if he had taken *Shabbat* seriously enough, if it had held the proper significance for him, he would not have forgotten it. One simply does not forget something once it reaches a certain level of importance in the mind.

Similarly, when we ask God to "remember" His covenant, and the merit of Abraham, Isaac, and Jacob, it is meant that those merits should become significant to Him. As mentioned earlier, on Rosh Hashanah everything returns to its original state. In its true state, everything is essentially without significance, and it is necessary to create this through our recitation of the verses of the Torah. The theme of the day becomes asking God to allow us to be significant, and thus the holiday is named "the Day of Remembrance."[31]

The recitation of *shofrot* along with the blowing of the *shofar* in spiritual service from the essence of the soul reaches God's essence.[32] This enables us to understand the details of the composition, sound, and other aspects of the *shofar*.

THE *SHOFAR*

The *shofar* is the horn of a ram. The sound is not musical, but rather an outcry, as we have explained, that represents the outcry of the return to God from the deepest part of the soul, deeper than words. The Ba'al Shem Tov gives the following parable for the meaning of *shofar*:

> There was a king who had a well-educated only child, who was dear to him, and who was truly the apple of his eye. The father decided that his son should travel to other countries to acquire knowledge and be exposed to the customs of different cultures. Therefore, he provided his son with ministers, servants, and great resources so that he could travel all over the world and reach a higher level of education than he had achieved at home. As time passed, the prince exhausted his treasury on the ex-

---

31. A mystical interpretation is that through the recitation of the verses of *zichronot* we elicit a spiritual level known as *soveiv kol almin*, a level of Godliness we are normally not significant enough to elicit (*Sefer Hama'amarim Melukat*, vol. 3, pp. 9–10).

32. Higher than the level known as *soveiv kol almin*. *Sefer Hama'amarim Melukat*, ibid.

penses of the journey and maintaining the level of luxury he was used to. More importantly, he acquired many new desires on his travels and spent freely on those until he ended up selling everything he owned. By that time he was in a far-away country where even his father, the King, was not known at all. So when he said that he was the son of King Such-and-Such, not only was he not believed, but his father's name was not even recognized. When he realized that, to his great distress, he was totally without any means of supporting himself, he decided to return to his father's country.

However, because so many years had elapsed, he had even forgotten his native language. What could he do, not even knowing the language? He made signs to others that he was the son of the king, but he was ridiculed by them. How could he be the noble prince, the son of the king, when he was so disheveled? They pummeled him on the head until he was covered with sores and bruises. Finally he reached the king's court, where he again gestured that he was the prince. Again, no one believed him until he cried out loudly so that the king would recognize his voice. When the king heard his voice, he said, "Is this not the voice of my son crying in distress?" His love for his son was aroused and he hugged him and kissed him.

The meaning of this parable is that the souls of the Jewish people are called God's children, even though God has no brother or son, strictly speaking. Nevertheless, God cherishes the Jewish people and calls them "children," as it is written, "My son, My firstborn, Israel,"[33] and also "You are children to the Lord, your God."[34] The soul "descends" into a body and this is analogous to

---

33. Exodus 4:22.
34. Deuteronomy 14:1.

the son traveling far away to further his education, i.e., through performing *mitzvot* and good deeds the soul reaches a higher level than it occupied previously. However, through love of one's own body and desire for wealth and the other things that humans desire, through being totally immersed in physicality, the soul becomes so distant that "it is in a place where the father's name is not recognized."[35] Through this distance the soul completely forgets everything it was accustomed to in its prior state, and it lacks everything both spiritually and physically. Forgetting the language in the parable means that the soul forgets its natural cleaving to Godliness, until the son begins to return and cry out in a simple voice that his father should recognize him. This is the sounding of the *shofar*, which is an inner cry from the depth of the heart expressing regret for the past and a good resolution for the future on the son's part to listen to the voice of his Father. Through this cry the King of kings is aroused, showing his love for His only son and forgives him for everything in the past. This forgiveness is the theme of Yom Kippur, which presents the opportunity for man to purify himself and be worthy of being forgiven by God. Then Sukkot follows with God's hugging of His children.[36]

What is particularly stressed in the Ba'al Shem Tov's parable is that the *shofar* is the cry of the child saying, "Father, father, save me." The Jewish people's cry from the depths of the soul reaches the essence of God and causes God to accept kingship and allows them to be His servants once again.

---

35. As we shall see in the chapter on *Pesach*, spiritual alienation is called *Mitzraim* (Egypt) which is etymologically related to *meitzarim*, limitations or straits. In connection with this we can observe that Pharoah stated, "Who is God that I should listen to His voice—I don't know God" (Exodus 5:2).

36. *Keter Shem Tov*, Additions, no. 108, pp. 193–194.

The sound of the *shofar* is a simple sound that awakens the simple part of the soul, which has no form. In turn, the simple level of the soul is one with the simple essence of God. The *shofar* does not have a delightful sound, and on the contrary, it awakens a feeling of trembling, as did the blowing of the *shofar* at the revelation of Sinai.

Rabbi Levi Yitzchak of Berditchev offers a different parable for the *shofar*:[37]

A king was traveling in a forest and lost his way. There were rustic people in the forest and he asked them the way back to his palace, but they did not recognize him and could not answer his question. One of the people in the forest was a wise man, who recognized the king and showed him the way back, bringing him to the palace and setting him again upon the royal throne. In gratitude the king made him a high official. Many days later, the man committed some offence against the king, and the king was very angry with him. He ordered the high officials of his government to judge him according to the law of a rebel. The man became very frightened, for he knew the judgement was going to be harsh, as befitted his crime. He fell down before the king and pleaded for his life, begging that before judgement he should be granted one request. He asked to be allowed to wear the clothes that he wore when he showed the king the way out of the forest and that the king should also put on the clothes he wore then. When the clothes were put on, the king remembered the great kindness that the man had shown him in leading him back to his palace and setting him on his throne, and his mercy was aroused for the

---

37. *Kudushat Levi, Derush Lerosh Hashanah*, entry beginning "*Bechatzotzerot*."

man. He then forgave him for his crime and restored him to his position.

The man in the parable signifies the Jewish people. At the time of the giving of the Torah God asked all the nations of the world to accept the Torah, but they declined. The Jewish people, however, accepted with joy and said *"Na'aseh venishmah"*—"We will do and we will hear."[38] We accepted the yoke of heaven and crowned God as King over us, to fulfill His laws and statutes. On Rosh Hashanah, after we have sinned during the year, we "wear the clothes that we wore then," and we blow the *shofar*, just as the *shofar* sounded at the giving of the Torah. When God remembers this merit, He forgives all of our sins, and inscribes us for a good life in the coming year.

The difference between the two parables is as follows: The first stresses the act of repentance of the Jerwish people, that they repent and cry out in a simple voice and accept the yoke of heaven. The second stresses God's remembrance of the excellence of the Jewish people that was revealed at the giving of the Torah. Both the act of repentance and remembrance are accomplished through the blowing of the *shofar*.[39]

Chasidic philosophy asks, given that the idea of *shofar* is a return to God in the deepest way, beyond an expression of mere physical words, why then, is it necessary to use the physical horn of an animal, the "least-alive" (i.e., most inanimate) and lowest part of the animal? The answer is that we are trying to bring God's kingship all the way down from the highest level to the lowest of all worlds, the physical world, and therefore we use a physical *shofar*.

---

38. See chapter on *Shavuot*.
39. *Likkutei Sichot*, vol. 34, pp. 183–184.

There is another way of explaining why the innermost part of a person's soul has to be expressed in the lowest form of physical life, a ram's horn. We can ask the same question about *mitzvot* in general. If a mitzvah is an expression of God's exalted will, why does it involve something so lowly as physical objects?

The answer is that, in general, the highest forms of spirituality can only be expressed on the lowest levels. This can be explained as follows: A revelation of Godliness is never a true expression of God's essence because the revelation has some particular character or quality and God's essence is absolutely pure and removed from particular qualities. Therefore, it can only be expressed in the physical realm, which has no revelation whatsoever.

This can be illustrated by way of analogy. An extremely wise person who wants to express something too deep for words may sometimes use a physical gesture or look. The physical act of the mitzvah is thus rooted in the highest form of Godliness, and the highest level of repentance is expressed in the physical act of blowing the *shofar*.

On Rosh Hashanah, the blowing of the *shofar* actually has three dimensions: the mitzvah of blowing the *shofar*, the association of blowing the *shofar* with repentance, and the association of the *shofar* with God's choice of the Jewish people.

The blowing of *shofar* as a mitzvah obviously does not suffice to cause God to accept the kingship and respond accordingly since we don't have the significance to even be given commandments. In other words, if a *basis* for being given *mitzvot* is what we are seeking on Rosh Hashanah, then a mitzvah itself will not elicit it. The second dimension in *shofar* is the outcry of the child returning to his father and begging him to be accepted once again. The idea of a child asking to be accepted implies a prior state of rebellion, and this requires repentance. However, if on Rosh Hashanah God's delight withdraws and the special relationship between God and the Jewish people needs to be renewed, as we have been saying, then we don't have any significance whatsoever to ask to be forgiven or accepted. Thus, the third dimension of *shofar* is that it transcends its status as a mitzvah and transcends the aspect of repentance. The blowing of the *shofar* brings God to once again choose the Jewish people, so that they will again be significant to Him, like a child to his father, and like a servant to a king.

Chasidic philosophy explains the concept of the chosen people, emphasizing that choice is beyond reason, emotion, or any other cause, for then it is not really a choice, but based on another factor. An important implication of this is that only God truly has free choice. This can explained in two ways: 1) Since God is the "Cause of all causes" and thus the Cause of any reason or rational, then He cannot be influenced by any such consideration, since He is logically prior to it. 2) Everything is truly insignificant to God since He is infinitely exalted beyond all other existence. Therefore, nothing has any significance with respect to God that would enable it to influence His choice.

Thus, once God chooses, the decision is based solely on His essence, and therefore it is without limits. When He does choose, the connection is stronger than any relationship whatsoever, even than that of a father to his child.

The three dimensions of blowing the *shofar* ultimately have three different accomplishments. The mitzvah of *shofar* accomplishes the necessary response from God, just as a servant who gives his master pleasure as a result of his service to him. The second aspect of *shofar* is the outcry of a child returning to his father, thus causing an even greater and deeper response from Him than before the child transgressed. Both are only possible, however, through the third dimension of *shofar,* which creates the connection to the essence of God (who is beyond any will or delight, so that the only word that applies is "choice"). Then we are once again chosen by God. This is why, before the sounding of the *shofar*, we recite the 47th Psalm, containing the verse "He *chooses* our heritage for us."[40]

Rosh Hashanah surpasses even the idea of *teshuvah*, and Rosh Hashanah is, thus, considered even above being a part of the Ten Days of Repentance.[41] It creates the connection of the Jewish people to God as the chosen people, which causes God to take pleasure in our service and to once again be King of the Universe.

In the prayers of Rosh Hashanah, when we refer to God in terms of Kingship and ruling, we are not simply referring to the spiritual renewal of His Kingship. We say, "And You shall rule" and "Rule over the whole world," and from the depths of our hearts we cry out *"Hamelech"*—"the King." We are asking for an extension of the scope of His kingship until "every created thing will understand that You created it."[42] Thus, the ultimate expression of the theme of kingship on Rosh Hashanah is our request that God's kingship will reach the ultimate revelation of the days of *Mashiach*.

---

40. Psalms 47:5.
41. This is also true of Yom Kippur. See discussion in that chapter.
42. Liturgy, *Amidah* for Rosh Hashanah.

3

 srp

Yom Kippur:
A Day of Delight

"For on this day He will atone for you, to cleanse you; you shall be clean from all your sins before God."   (Leviticus 16:30)

The epigraph verse to this chapter encapsulates the spiritual content of the day of Yom Kippur. As we have been explaining, each Jewish holiday is not just a commemoration of something that occurred in the past, but a spiritual reoccurrence. The event that reoccurs on Yom Kippur is God's forgiveness of the Jewish people for the sin of the golden calf and the consequent giving of the second tablets. In the above verse, the phrase "He will atone for you" does not mention by name the One who is granting the atonement. The reason is that the atonement of Yom Kippur involves a revelation of God's essence, which is higher than any designation or appellation. Similarly, the phrase *"lifnei Hashem"* is normally translated as "before God" (i.e., in the presence of God).

However, "*lifnei*" can also mean "before" in the sense of "preceding" as something higher can be said to precede something lower in a hierarchy. On Yom Kippur we connect to God's essence, a level that is "before" or that transcends the level designated by the Tetragrammaton, God's unique, ineffable Name.[1] The vessel for achieving this connection is through the Jewish people's turning to God in *teshuvah*—usually translated as "repentance," but more accurately translated as "returning"—and therefore we will begin by examining the act of *teshuvah*.

Rabbi Schneur Zalman of Liadi in *Igeret Hateshuvah* defines the basic meaning of the mitzvah of *teshuvah* as follows:

> The commandment of repentance as required by the Torah is simply the abandonment of sin. . . . One must resolve in perfect sincerity never to revert to folly to rebel against God's rule. One will never again violate one of the King's commands, whether positive or negative.[2]

Once a person does *teshuvah*, his sins are not even mentioned in Heaven when he is judged after he passes away. We might wonder how *teshuvah* can accomplish so much. Why is it possible to erase the past, so to speak? The answer is that *teshuvah* essen-

---

1. In this case the four letters of God's name represent His attributes. Throughout the year, every mitzvah relates to one of the letters of God's name, thereby determining the character of our general relationship with Him. On Yom Kippur, however, one connects to the essence of God *before* He channels and condenses himself through the letters of His name, i.e., a level higher than such expression.

2. *Tanya, Igeret Hateshuvah* p. 91. It is interesting to note that this particular formulation has a novel aspect compared to that of other authorities: in contrast to simply requiring that one renounce a particular sin, Rabbi Schneur Zalman speaks of promising never to rebel again by violating *any* positive or negative commandment.

tially relates to a level of connection that is higher than *mitzvot*, as we will explore. To understand what is required to accomplish true, whole-hearted repentence, we must consider the inner dimension of repentence.

TESHUVAH AS RETURN

This resolve not to rebel against the commandments of the King is nevertheless merely the external dimension of repentence. The inner dimension of *teshuvah* is discussed extensively in chasidic philosophy. In order to understand this, we must first consider the unique existence of a Jewish person. According to the Torah, when God created Adam's body from the earth, He "blew a living soul into his nostrils."[3] God, in contrast, used "utterances,"[4] divine speech, to create all other creations. The *Zohar* explains about the word "blowing" that "one who blows must blow from deep within."[5] Thus, the Jewish soul[6] has an intimate relationship with God that is not possesed by any other created entity. The loftiness of the source of the Jewish soul gives it an even deeper relationship with God than even that of angels, who were also created through "utterances." Another implication of the contrasting terms "uttering" and "blowing" is that speaking is not subject to being blocked. When a person speaks to another, an intervening object does not cause any interference, but when a person

---

3. Genesis 2:7.

4. Such as "Let there be light" (Genesis 1:3).

5. Not in current printed editons of the *Zohar*, see *Tanya*, ch. 2.

6. Although Adam is the progenitor of all mankind, chasidic philosophy explains that Adam's soul is the "comprehensive soul" that includes all the souls of the Jewish people.

blows onto something, even the slightest obstructon will block the path of the breath.

When a person transgresses a God-given commandment, he creates an obstruction between himself and God[7]; therefore, what is really at stake is the Jew's special relationship with God. Unless the Jew does *teshuvah* after sinning, he must exist with the same spiritual "energy" as any other creation on earth. For the soul, the severing of its previous intimate relationship with God is tremendous suffering.

The person must evoke the part of his soul that remains unblemished and loyal to God. This enables us to reach out to God Himself, to a level deeper, as it were, than His desire for this or that commandment.[8] God then responds to our act of *teshuvah* by reopening the circuit of our connection to Him and causing the "flow" of spiritual current to return to its original state. *Teshuvah*, then, means re-establishing the very special relationship one has with God, one based on the "inner breath." In contrast to the usual mournful associations of *teshuvah*, *teshuvah* actually has an extremely upbeat aspect: The soul experiences a joyous homecoming. In order to further understand the unique accomplishment of Yom Kippur, we must first explore the different levels of *teshuvah* as discussed in Chasidic philosophy.

"LOWER *TESHUVAH*" AND "HIGHER *TESHUVAH*"

"*Teshuvah tata'ah*"—"lower *teshuvah*"—is the term used in chasidic philosophy when referring to repentence following sins,

---

7. This obstruction is only in terms of how much the person receives from God; God never actually leaves him.

8. The level known as "*Ba'al Haratzon*" in chasidic terminology.

restoring the severed connection to God by arousing God's mercy on the soul that has fallen so low and humbling oneself by contemplating the degradation that has been imposed on the soul.[9] The focus is on returning through counteracting and abandoning the negative. *"Teshuvah ila'ah"*—"higher *teshuvah*"—is essentially the return of the transgressor's soul to its source, God's infinite light, the level on which it existed before descending to become clothed in a body.[10] This type of *teshuvah* is a return to the original state of never having left God in the first place, and it pertains, as Chasidic philosophy explains in many places, even to righteous people who never lose their connection to God.[11] Even though God's flow of "breath" is never interrupted for the *tzaddik*, his soul does not have the intimate relationship it had in heaven before coming down into a body. This relationship is related to God's "breath" before being "blown," as it were.[12] Rabbi Schneur Zalman of Liadi writes the following of "higher *teshuvah*":

> "[the penitent] through meditating on the greatness of God with all the profundity of his intellect, arouses a sense of intellectual reverence and love." "This love," he continues, "is primarily the cleaving of spirit to spirit . . . this cleaving of spirit is the meaning of "[You shall love the Lord, your God] with all your soul. . . ."[13]

When a person achieves this love, he is motivated to unite all his faculties with God. He studies Torah, uniting his intellect with

---

9. *Igeret Hateshuvah*, ch. 7.

10. *Likkutei Torah, Acharei* 25a; see also *Likkutei Torah, Ha'azinu*, 71c.

11. *Torah Or, Vayechi*, 45a.

12. This level of "breath" is referred to by the traditional phrasing *"hevel shebelev"*—literally "the breath of the heart."

13. Deuteronomy 6:5.

God, he speaks words of *halachah*, uniting his faculty of speech with God, and he does deeds of kindness, "thus cleaving to God's actions."[14] In contrast to *teshuvah tata'ah*, which focuses on correcting the negative, *teshuvah ila'ah* especially emphasizes the joyful aspect of *teshuvah* since the whole emphasis is the soul's return to its source.

The restoration of our relationship with God prior to the soul's embodiment seems to be a lofty aspiration; nevertheless, the concept of returning to one's source is an inner motivation for the most basic act of *teshuvah*, when one promises not to rebel. However, an act of *teshuvah* always expresses a deeper dimension of which the penitent person may not be consciously aware. Beyond the paradox that *teshuvah* is also relevant to the righteous who never sin, we thus discover the seemingly even more paradoxical relevance of this level of *teshuvah* to every Jew, whatever his spiritual status.

This higher level of *teshuvah* is relevant the whole year, and especially on *Shabbat*,[15] but it is the central theme of Yom Kippur. After the service of God in the month of Elul and the days of *Selichot* and the Ten Days of *Teshuvah*, which are all included in the process of doing *teshuvah tata'ah*, one reaches Yom Kippur, whose theme is *teshuvah ila'ah* in a joyful mode.[16]

---

14. *Tanya, Igeret Hateshuvah*, ch. 9.

15. *Shabbat* has the same letters as *tasheiv* and the spiritual service of *Shabbat* is to return the soul to God.

16. If so, why do we constantly confesss and talk about our sins on Yom Kippur? The reason is that once we reach the higher level of *teshuvah*, returning to our source, our past *teshuvah* is not sufficient, and therefore we go back and correct our mistakes again, this time through *teshuvah ila'ah*, which is in a joyful mode.

THE ESSENCE OF THE DAY ATONES

Beyond the special emphasis on the higher levels of *teshuvah*, Yom Kippur embodies an infinitely higher concept, which ultimately relates to the essence of the Jewish soul and its relationship to God's essence.

To understand this, however, we must return again to the subject of sin. The Talmud states that when a person transgresses a positive commandment (for example, by failing to eat *matzah* on the night of *Pesach*), and then repents, he is immediately forgiven.[17] However, if he violates a negative commandment, even if he immediately repents, he must wait until Yom Kippur to be forgiven. It is also understood that violating God's command, which is active, is worse than failing to obey a positive command, which is passive. Violating a negative commandment, thus, obviously has more severe consequences spiritually than omitting a positive commandment. Chasidic philosophy explains on a deeper level that the violator of a negative commandment stains, or blemishes, his soul, and thus damages the spiritual world to which he is connected, his soul's source.

The purpose of positive commandments is to increase Godliness in the world, and failing to observe a positive commandment deprives the world of the additional light, but does not blemish the soul. This is why forgiveness for violating a positive commandment does not have to wait until Yom Kippur, while correcting a blemish requires the power of "the Holy Day," as Yom Kippur is sometimes called.[18] This leads us to a new question. Why exactly

---

17. *Yoma* 86a.

18. On the other hand, chasidic philosophy explains that the main purpose for human existence in the world is to increase spiritual light

does Yom Kippur have the ability to repair the blemishes to the soul?

There are actually different levels in a Jew's connection to God. One level is the connection through fulfilling *mitzvot* and accepting the yoke of Heaven. A Jew undertakes to fulfill whatever God commands, and this establishes a certain relationship. Through sinning, a Jew severs this connection, as we explained above. When he does so, he is likely to feel remorse and pain.

Given that the soul is made up different levels, a Jew's regret after sinning indicates that there is a level that is deeper than the connection through fulfilling *mitzvot*. The sinner has severed the connection based on fulfilling commandments, and therefore this higher level is the only possible cause for his regret and it is revealed when the person does *teshuvah*. On this level a Jew is con-

---

through performing *mitzvot*. Creating blemishes is merely something to be avoided. This is why a positive commandment overrides a negative one if the same act involves both a fulfillment of a command and a violation of a prohibition. For instance, some aspects of circumcision violate *Shabbat*, but we nevertheless carry out a circumcision on the eighth day of a boy's life. From this standpoint, the spiritual energy that was omitted by not observing a positive commandment is more significant than the fact that violating a prohibition transgresses against God's will. Therefore ordinary *teshuvah* cannot make up the missing light. The fact that a person is immediately forgiven if he repents only applies to the fact that he rebelled against God by not listening to His commands. However, the light that would have been revealed in the world is not recovered. The *Mishnah* (*Berachot* 26a) applies the phrase "something crooked that cannot be made straight" (Ecclesiastes 1:5) in reference to violating a positive command and gives the example of someone neglecting to say the *Shema* at night. However, chasidic philosophy explains that Yom Kippur can even make up for the missing light of the past year.

nected to God as He is higher than clothing His will in any particular mitzvah.[19]

As lofty as this connection is, the fact that it expresses itself specifically in an impulse toward *teshuvah* indicates that it is limited in having a particular form. Higher still is the connection between the essence of the soul and God's essence. This connection is completely unlimited and too lofty to be expressed as any impulse, even the impulse to do *teshuvah*. There is no spiritual service or sin that can have any positive or negative effect on it since all action performed by human beings are of necessity limited. The special accomplishment of Yom Kippur is that this connection is revealed, and thus any blemishes are instantly dispelled, since blemishes have no relevance to this level whatsoever. This is what is meant by the Talmud's statement, "*Itzumo shel yom mechapeir*"—"The essence of the day atones."[20]

The essence of Yom Kippur goes beyond even the return of the soul to the state of never having left God. God's essential relationship with the Jewish people utterly transcends *teshuvah*, and God as He is completely removed and exalted reveals His love and the absolute oneness that exists between Him and the Jewish nation. In this feeling of unity with God on Yom Kippur, stemming from an expression of the deeper essence of the soul, one cannot even speak of transgression or being detached from God, for the highest part of the soul remains one with God at all times.

---

19. This level of Godliness is called *Ba'al Haratzon* in chasidic philosophy.

20. *Shevu'ot* 13a. In the well-known disagreement between Rabbi Yehudah Hanasi and the Sages concerning whether atonement requires repentence, both sides agree that "the essence of the day atones." The disagreement concerns whether repentence is a pre-condition (the position of the Sages) or not (*Likkutei Sichot*, vol. 4, pp. 1149–1150).

Throughout the day of Yom Kippur, the feeling is not so much one of reconnecting but rather of never having left.

On a day of such spiritual delight as Yom Kippur it is clear that not eating on this day must have a different character than the mournful fasting and deprivation of a fast day. The usual explanation of fasting is that we give our flesh and blood as a sacrifice to God, with the added benefit of gaining more humility and sensitivity to spiritual values. Sometimes after a person repents, he observes a private fast day on which his sacrifice of flesh and blood helps complete the process of correction for a sin. There are two stages: forgiveness and atonement. After a person repents and is forgiven, he still needs atonement, the restoration of his former relationship to God. The fast itself is compared to a gift given to an earthly king against whom one has rebelled. After the rebellion has been forgiven, the subject may give the king a gift because he still lacks his former favor with the king, a state in which the king delights in his service.

Chasidic philosophy understands the fasting on Yom Kippur, in contrast, as the body reaching a high level at which it lives solely from Godliness, so that there is no need for food or other physical needs. Chasidic philosophy explains the phrase *ulechayotam bera'av* (to keep them alive during a time of hunger)[21] to mean that a person literally derives life and sustenance *bera'av*—"from hunger"—i.e., from fasting on Yom Kippur.[22] Instead of the nourishment derived from eating and drinking, he is sustained from the matters of holiness in which he is involved.[23]

---

21. Psalms 33:19.

22. *Likkutei Torah, Shir Hashirim* 14b.

23. According to another explanation, the life of the body generally comes from the inanimate, vegetable, and animal matter a person consumes. On a fast day, however, the food that the person consumed the

It is possible to think that Yom Kippur is a grim and morose day. We are dressed in white garments, which, according to one explanation, resemble burial shrouds. We fast and minimize physical comforts (such as bathing), and after every prayer service we pound ourselves on the chest, proclaiming "We have transgressed, we have acted perfidiously. . . ." Even the phrase "Yom Kippur"— "Day of Atonement"—has a negative connotation, since atonement, seemingly, is only relevant to someone who has sinned. Paradoxically, Yom Kippur is the most supremely uplifting holiday in the Jewish calendar, a day on which the soul derives a profound inner gratification.

On the deepest level, on Yom Kippur we gain the potential to live solely from the delight of being one with God.[24] This is an absolutely pure delight which is uncombined even with other types of spiritual delight, such as that of fulfilling a mitzvah. Along the same lines, we can also understand why Yom Kippur is called "*Shabbat Shabbaton*"—(the Sabbath of all Sabbaths). As chasidic philosophy explains, the theme of *Shabbat* is the return of the soul to its source.[25] On Yom Kippur, a Jew has the ability to make the ultimate return: back to his essence—his *yechidah*.

During the year *teshuvah* is a means by which the Jewish people gain forgiveness and return to their source, but on Yom Kippur

---

day before has already reached a higher level by being incorporated into the physical make-up of a human being. The person thus derives even his physical life in the ordinary sense from a higher level than usual (*Likkutei Sichot*, vol. 33, p. 160).

24. This is comparable to Moses's not eating when he was on Mount Sinai for forty days receiving the Torah. This state will also be experienced in the period of the resurrection of the dead, when souls will be in bodies but nevertheless live off spirituality.

25. Rearranged, the letters of the word "*Shabbat*" spell the word "*tasheiv*," which means "return." See the chapter on *Shabbat*.

teshuvah is merely a prerequisite and a vessel for the essence of the day to penetrate. Yom Kippur, like Rosh Hashanah, is essentially above being counted as one of the Ten Days of Repentance, as indicated by the Talmud's references to the days of repentance being between Rosh Hashanah and Yom Kippur. Actually, there are only seven days between Rosh Hashanah and Yom Kippur, and the Days of Awe plus the seven make up the number ten. However, the reference to the ten days being between Rosh Hashanah and Yom Kippur indicates a dimension of these two holidays that transcends the Ten Days of Repentance.[26]

When the highest level of unity with God is revealed on Yom Kippur, the soul transcends the limitations of the body and the world. The revelation of the essence of the day brings this even to the soul in its own limits. Thus, the essence of Yom Kippur surpasses the highest form of *teshuvah*, and that is why it is not counted in the Ten Days of Repentence.

Therefore, when this fact is revealed to us, there is nothing we do, or fail to do, that can affect our relationship with God. This is why the power of the day of Yom Kippur can correct and remove blemishes from the spiritual attributes of the soul. When that enormous love is revealed, any stain becomes insignificant, and the "light" of Yom Kippur makes up for all "missing light." Thus, despite repentance being a prerequisite for Yom Kippur to reveal this connection, what this day accomplishes far exceeds man's efforts.

Now that we have stressed the holiness of Yom Kippur that transcends repentence, we might wonder why it is nevertheless called "The Day of Atonement," which seems to emphasize the correction of the damage caused by sin. The explanation is that the atonement itself, in its simple sense, reveals the infinite

---

26. *Likkutei Sichot*, vol. 4, p. 1149 and ff.

strength of the bond of the Jewish people and God. Even when the Jewish people do the opposite of God's will, through *teshuvah* and the day of Yom Kippur they recover their intimate relationship with God as if they have never sinned.[27]

THE FIVE LEVELS OF THE SOUL

Just as on Yom Kippur the essence of God's love is revealed to the Jewish people, on that day the essence of our soul is revealed to God. Many sources in Chasidic philosophy discuss at great depth the five levels of the soul.[28] From the lowest to the highest they are *nefesh* (associated with action), *ruach* (associated with emotions), *neshamah* (associated with intellect), *chayah* (associated with the will—the soul as it is moving towards a goal), and *yechidah* (associated with delight—the soul, not as it is moving towards a goal, but as it exists for itself, in its essence). *Yechidah* is the level of the soul that is always united with God and that stays attached to Him and loyal to Him. The name *yechidah* derives from an attribute of God, that He called "*Yachid*"[29]: absolutely singular and unique. The *yechidah* is connected to and reveals that level of Godliness.

Throughout the year, one functions with the three lower levels, considered mere reflections of the soul: the *nefesh* is used to perform *mitzvot*, the *ruach* feels love and fear of God, and the *neshamah* enables the person to meditate on God's greatness. On Yom Kippur, however, the theme of the day is to relate to God

---

27. *Sefer Hama'amarim* 5737, "*Shuvah Yisrael.*"

28. *Bereshit Rabbah* 14, 60; *Devarim Rabbah* 2, 37.

29. *Sefer Hama'amarim* 5688, "*Ashreinu.*"

through one's *yechidah*. This is why Yom Kippur is the only day of the year on which there are five different prayer services, as underscored by the language of the Sages that Yom Kippur is "the day when we are obligated in five prayers."[30] Each of the first four prayer services allows the *yechidah* to penetrate one of the four other levels of the soul. In the fifth, *Ne'ilah*, *yechidah* is revealed in its purity. The revelation of the level of *yechidah* of the soul and the corresponding revelation of God's transcendent unity is the mystical dimension of the principle discussed above that the "the essence of the day atones."

The souls of the Jewish people collectively are also divided according to the five levels of the soul. On Yom Kippur, the High Priest, who is called "the *yechidah* of the Jewish people,"[31] does all the services in the holy Temple. This level of absolute unity is expressed in every aspect of the holiday: The only time when it was permitted to enter the Holy of Holies was on Yom Kippur, for the Holy of Holies was the single, unique place where the essence of God's holiness was revealed. So, too, in time, the day of Yom Kippur is *achat beshanah* (once in a year).[32] Out of the 365 days of the year, it is the one day on which evil has no power. Thus, on Yom Kippur *yechidah* is expressed in time, in space, and in the person performing the service.[33]

---

30. *Likkutei Torah* 81b.

31. There is also a concept of a *yechidah haklaliut*, a general *yechidah*, which is *Mashiach*. Just as the *Kohain Gadol* was the *yechidah* of the Jewish people during the time of the Temple, the Jewish people in all generations are divided into five general levels, with *Mashiach* representing the *yechidah*.

32. Exodus 30:10.

33. *Sefer Yetzirah* explains that every entity has the three aspects of *olam*—"world" (i.e., place), *shanah*—"year" (i.e., time), and *nefesh*—"soul."

On Yom Kippur the High Priest would burn incense in the Holy of Holies. The word for "incense" in Hebrew is *ketoret*, which is related to the word for "knot." Just as two things can be firmly tied together, the *ketoret* united the Jewish people with God in the deepest way possible.

Along the same lines, chasidic philosophy expounds on the clothes the *Kohain Gadol* (High Priest) wore when he entered the Holy of Holies. Throughout the year, the *Kohain Gadol* wore special garments made of threads of gold, including a breast-plate that bore valuable gems. However, on Yom Kippur, when he went into the Holy of Holies, he wore plain white garments of pure linen.

Why, in the holiest place on earth, did the *Kohain Gadol* wear only pure white linen, and not the jewel-bedecked garments that he wore otherwise? The color white represents purity and essence.[34] The golden garments represent the highest expression of the ten faculties of the soul of the Jew throughout the year. The central theme of Yom Kippur, however, is the unity of God's essence and the Jew's essence, which is pure and not subject to blemish.

For that reason, on Yom Kippur all Jewish people unite and God relates to all equally. When the Jews' relationship to God is based on their conduct and observance, then it differs according to the level of each person. However, the forgiveness of Yom Kippur, through the revelation of God's love for us, is far beyond what we do or don't do. On that level, we are all God's children equally. This is why, immediately before *Kol Nidre* services, we say "we hereby grant permission to pray with those who have transgressed," uniting with all Jews, even the gravest transgressors.

---

34. See *Or Hatorah, Derushim LeSukkot*, pp. 1717–1718.

This was also emphasized in the times of the Temple by the *Kohain Gadol* as he entered the Holy of Holies and offered eleven different kinds of incense combined together. One of the components of the incense, *chelbenah*, had an unpleasant odor. However, when it was mixed with the other ten components, it became tolerable. The *Kohain Gadol* was obligated to use *chelbenah* in the Holy of Holies, and if he omitted it, the incense would not be acceptable as an offering and he would be committing a grave sin. Why was a bad-smelling spice use in the *ketoret*? The answer is that the incense represented bringing all Jews, including the sinful, the spiritually malodorous, into the Holy of Holies—uniting all Jews equally.

Chasidic philosophy explains that holiness is associated with the number ten while the symbol of impurity is the number eleven. The reason for this is that forces of impurity, like all created entities, need a force of Godliness to keep them in existence. Unlike holiness, which is generally associated with inwardness, making a vessel—impurity can never be a vessel for Godly energy. It can only live off an energy that doesn't need a vessel.[35] Since the life-force of impurity is not a part of it, being counted separately, the life-force of impurity plus the ten forces of holiness from which it derives nurture is represented by a one added to ten.

This is the meaning of the service of the *Kohain Gadol* in the Holy of Holies on Yom Kippur. Burning incense and making smoke subdues and elevates the forces of impurity because the cloud, which surrounds the *Kohain Gadol*, represents the inner

---

35. Impurity actually derives nurture from two different life-forces. One is a life-force that is so contracted and diminished that it does not need a vessel. The other is an extremely lofty life-force that is essentially beyond being enclothed in a vessel.

aspect of the level of Godliness known as the "encompassing light," God's inner delight.[36]

Our discussion of the five levels of the soul allows us to add a dimension to our earlier explanation of why Yom Kippur is called "The Day of Atonement," a name which does not seem to stress the holiness of the day. The repair of blemishes in the lower levels of the soul *nefesh, ruach,* and *neshamah* has an advantage over the revelation of the essence of the soul, which is never blemished, since the lower levels achieve atonement *despite* the fact that they can become blemished. They have the advantage of *overcoming* blemishes. Moreover, the revelation of the essence of the soul reveals that in the essence of each of the lower levels[37] there was also never any blemish and this, too, is a greater accomplishment than simply the revelation of the soul's essence.[38]

THE TWO GOATS

Another central observance of Yom Kippur in Temple times was the lottery of the *shnei se'irim* (two goats). The *Mishnah*[39] tells us

---

36. The smoke in the Holy of Holies resembles a cloud, and the *sukkah* similarly symbolizes the clouds of glory that surrounded the Jews on all sides when they traveled in the desert. Thus, the symbolism of the encompassing light is also associated with Sukkot, when we take this encompassing light that was elicited on Yom Kippur and "bring it down" to have an inner effect on the Jewish people. Implicit in the use of the word "encompassing" is the concept that this light is infinite. Since normally it is too lofty to be absorbed inwardly, it remains "encompassing" or "surrounding."

37. The essence of each of the lower levels is the same as the essence of the soul in general, since that exists on all levels.

38. *Sefer Hama'amarim* 5737, "*Shuvah Yisrael.*"

39. *Yoma* 62a.

that on Yom Kippur two goats, identical in every way, were designated for two different services. One goat was offered on the altar as a sacrifice to God, and all the sins of the Jewish people were placed on the other, the scapegoat, which was pushed off a cliff. The question arises concerning the need for two *identical* goats. The scapegoat, we might think, does not need to be as perfect as if it is also being offered on the altar, but the Torah states that the two goats are to be identical so that the only way to choose between them is a lottery.

Yom Kippur, considering its observance in Temple times, is thus directly related to the idea of lottery. The *Tikkunei Zohar* states that the name "*Purim*" derives from the talmudic term for Yom Kippur, "*Yom Ki-pur-rim*," which can be interpreted as a "A Day like *Purim*."[40] Rabbi Schneur Zalman makes the related statement that *Yom Hakipurim* is "like *Purim*."[41] Rabbi Schneur Zalman's statement, which cites *Purim* to explain the name of Yom Kippur, rather than the other way around, especially underscores that the connection beween *Purim* and Yom Kippur indicated by the *Tikkunei Zohar* relates to the essence of Yom Kippur.[42] The translation of the word "*Purim*" is "lots," so that the entire holiday is named after the idea of a lottery. Chasidic philosophy explains that a lottery involves equal and random choices. The spiritual meaning of a lottery is that from the level of infinity, everything is equal, so that God is infinitely and equally removed from everything, while also being equally close to everything. In the same way, the *yechidah*, the essence of our soul, is also called the "lot" of the soul. It is infinitely removed from mundane existence, and at the same time the *yechidah* is expressed even on the lowest level

40. *Tikkunei Zohar* 421 (57b).
41. *Torah Or* 121a.
42. See *Sefer Hama'amarim Melukat*, vol. 5, p. 189, note 9.

of action, in a person's physical performance of a mitzvah. Therefore, to emphasize the connection between the "lot" of the soul and the infinity of God, the goats are chosen by drawing lots.

The idea of a lottery emphasizes God's choice of the Jewish people, which is revealed on Yom Kippur. The essential idea of choice is that there is no compulsion to choose one way or another. When one thing has an advantage over the other, then there is an intellectual "compulsion," so to speak, in the choice, since only one choice makes sense over the other. Therefore, it is only God's essence, the level that is infinitely exalted so that no advantage or defect has any relevance, that truly chooses the Jewish people, since on that level God is utterly and equally exalted over everything, and everything is truly equal.[43] Such a choice, then, is similar to a lottery in which choice is made at random, i.e., in a completely uncompelled way. Thus, even if the Jewish people are in a state of iniquity, God's choice and essential love are not concealed, since the choice is not based on any advantageous quality in the Jewish people or any other factor, but on God Himself. His essence is thus revealed since it is expressed in the choice. When God's essence and God's essential love for and choice of the Jewish people are revealed on Yom Kippur, all achieve atonement.[44] Since this choice is based on God's essence and not on any advantageous quality of the Jewish people, it is a limitlessly powerful connection.

---

43. The emphasis on this level of Godliness, which is beyond names, explains why, as pointed out earlier, the first clause of the verse quoted at the beginning of this chapter does not mention God by name. Similarly, the Book of Esther, which we read on *Purim*, does not mention God by name.

44. In mystical terms, this level of Godliness is higher than *hishtalshelut*. This level is also revealed on *Purim*, thus adding a dimension to

VERBAL CONFESSION

On Yom Kippur, a good portion of every *Amidah* prayer is taken up with confession, which is essential to fulfilling the biblical commandment of repentance, even for one who has repented sincerely in his heart. Chasidic philosophy explains that by humbling ourselves through confession, we awaken mercy and compassion from above. In light of God's exaltedness, which is revealed on Rosh Hashanah, we acknowledge on Yom Kippur that even our most sincere service is insufficient to serve the King of kings. If it is inadequate, it is even considered rebellion to not render the proper service that befits God's greatness. Through our self-abasement in confession we evoke God's willingness to take pleasure in our service, not as a response to our service's intrinsic worth, but as an act of mercy.

One of the explanations given for the necessity to verbally specify the mistake and to ask for forgiveness is that it helps us concentrate and feel our repentance more deeply. The source of words is the deepest part of the soul, even deeper than the emotion itself. Therefore, words are able to draw down the loftiest spiritual "energy."[45]

---

our understanding of how *Yom Hakipurim* can be translated as "a day like *Purim.*"

45. This explanation can help us understand why it is not enough to feel regrets over mistakes and why one has to verbalize these regrets. However, it is still unclear why a person who feels true repentance but who doesn't verbalize has still not fulfilled the mitzvah according to Jewish law. The answer is that a mitzvah requires some action, and moving the lips in confession is considered a minor form of action (*Bava Metzia* 90b, *Sanhedrin* 65a).

Chasidic philosophy explains further that every human action, positive or negative, creates angels in the spiritual realm. The angels them-

Yom Kippur, then, is not at all to be understood as a mournful day on which we are consumed with our failures and transgressions; rather Yom Kippur is the most uplifting day of the year, a taste of the Messianic era, when the world will experience the ultimate revelation of Godliness and the Jewish people will feel the ultimate closeness to God. Because of the incredible highs of the day, a Jew does whatever he can to eliminate anything that stands in the way of this intimacy with the Divine. Yom Kippur is called the "Sabbath of all Sabbaths," and the world to come is called "that day which will be all *Shabbat*."[46] Just as in the period of resurrection when we will have physical bodies and nevertheless live from spirituality, the affliction of the body physically on Yom Kippur enables us to take delight in holiness and draw our sustenance from it. The true character of Yom Kippur is thus not only delight, but the ultimate delight.

---

selves are made up of a soul and a body. The body of an angel is, of course, much more spiritual than a human body. According to Jewish mysticism, a human body is composed of fire, water, air, and earth. By contrast, an angel's body is composed of only the more spiritual elements, fire and air. A person's feeling of enthusiasm while committing a sin creates the soul of a negative angel, and the actual act creates its body. Therefore, when a person repents, these two elements have to be eliminated. Since the angel was created with enthusiasm, the *feeling* of repentance and regret removes its soul. The body is removed by the actual verbalizing of confession, a physical act that uses part of the body—the lips—corresponding to the angel's body. Confession in prayer is arranged according to the Hebrew *alef-bet* so that we cover any possibility of sin, and thus all possibilities for the creation of negative angels, in our confessions. Moreover, everything that exists, including the negative, is created by combinations of the letters of the *alef-bet*, which are its source of life. Confession, using all the letters, takes away the "life-force" of the sin.

46. Psalm 92:1. See *Mishnah*, end tractate *Tamid*.

CHAPTER

4

ک

Sukkot: The King's Embrace

"You shall dwell in sukkot seven days, every native in Israel shall dwell in sukkot; that your descendants may know that I had the children of Israel dwell in sukkot when I brought them out of Egypt. . . ." (Leviticus 23:42–43)

AFTER THE DAYS OF AWE

The holiday of Sukkot is a direct continuation of Rosh Hashanah and Yom Kippur. This can be understood by continuing the Ba'al Shem Tov's analogy of the king and his son when explaining the Days of Awe. The reader will recall that the son had been away for many years and returned once again to his father. In terms of the holidays, the son's return to the king's palace and his renewed acceptance commences with Rosh Hashanah and culminates on

Yom Kippur. However, the love between God and the Jewish people that is manifested on Rosh Hashanah and Yom Kippur, while involving both of God's roles, King and father, mainly focuses on God's kingship, with the accompanying feeling of awe that this evokes. The next stage is the father embracing the child, revealing his fatherly love and enjoying his son's presence once again.

A verse in Psalms[1] also indicates the relationship between Rosh Hashanah and Sukkot: "Blow the *shofar* on the new moon on the designated day of our Holy Day." The Hebrew word *bakesseh* (designated) is related to the Hebrew word for "covering"—"*kisui.*" The Talmud[2] states that the holiday that is "hidden" is Rosh Hashanah because it is the beginning of the month and the moon is mostly hidden then. Sukkot falls on the fifteenth of the month, *Pesach* falls on the fifteenth of the month, and *Shavuot* on the sixth day of the month. The only holiday that begins when the moon is concealed is Rosh Hashanah.

Chasidic philosophy explains that the next two words, *leyom chageinu* (for our holiday) refer to Sukkot. Everything that begins on the "hidden day," Rosh Hashanah, is finally revealed when the moon is full (i.e., what happens spiritually on Rosh Hashanah and Yom Kippur is finally revealed on Sukkot).[3]

---

1. 81:4.

2. Rosh Hashanah 8b, *Beitzah* 16a.

3. This is also indicated by a well-known *Midrash*: "Rabbi Avin stated, the matter may be understood with a parable: it is like the case of two people who have come to a judge and about whom we do not know who has been victorious. But if one of them takes a palm branch in his hand we know that he has won. So it is with Israel and the nations of the world: The nations come and bring accusations before God on Rosh Hashanah and we do not know which has won. But since the Jewish people go forth

The Torah indicates that the reason for sitting in the *sukkah* on Sukkot is to remember that God surrounded the Jewish nation with clouds[4] to shield them from the sun's heat during the forty-year period they wandered in the desert. The clouds in the desert were not only physical protection from the elements but spiritually a manifestation of God's love. On Sukkot the *sukkah* also represents God's love ("hugging" in the analogy above). On Sukkot, then, there is a spiritual recurrence of what happened when the Jews originally travelled through the desert, and we once again experience God's love. This love is also a revelation of what happened on the Days of Awe as a result of our turning back to God.

On Rosh Hashanah every Jew must unite with every other Jew to accept God's kingship and serve God from the innermost depths of his soul, a level in which all are equal, no matter what their level of piety. In this unity, there is no recognition of differences or levels among Jews, all are equally servants of the King of kings.

After this unity is achieved on Rosh Hashanah, the Jewish people go on to achieve a higher level of unity on Sukkot. This higher level is the theme of the well-known symbolism of the four species, in which each one represents a different type of Jew. The *lulav*, which has a taste but not an aroma, represents one who learns Torah but who doesn't perform *mitzvot*, while the *etrog*, having a taste and an aroma, is one who learns Torah and also performs *mitzvot*. The myrtle, with an aroma but no taste, is one

---

from the presence of God bearing their *lulavim* and *etrogim* in their hands, we know that it is Israel who are victorious, that Israel were successful in the judgement and that their iniquities were pardoned . . ." (*Vayikra Rabbah* 30, 2).

4. According to the accepted opinion in *Sukkah* 11a.

who performs *mitzvot* and does not learn Torah, and the willow, having neither taste nor aroma, neither learns Torah nor performs *mitzvot*. The *Midrash* declares, "God said, 'bind them all together into one bundle, and each one will atone for the other.'"[5] Thus, the unity achieved by the Jewish people on Sukkot involves recognition of differences in level among Jews, though nevertheless they are unified. Therefore, unlike the unity of Rosh Hashanah, involving a level of the Jewish soul in which there are actually no differences, the unification of Sukkot is higher in its achievement of unity precisely from truly disparate elements.

MAKIF AND *PENIMI*

In order to understand the full significance of dwelling in the *sukkah* we must become familiar with a key concept in chasidic philosophy. Godliness can, generally speaking, be expressed in one of two ways, both of which are necessary for the existence of the world. In the first, Godliness is limited so that it can become revealed within a limited created entity, which is then referred to as a "vessel," something which can "contain" the revelation. When Godly creative force is revealed in this way it is called an *or penimi*—an inward light. The entity that is serving as the vessel feels this light inwardly. In the other mode of expression, Godly force is unlimited. It is then too lofty to be contained in a vessel, and it is said to "encompass" or "surround" that to which it becomes revealed. It is then called an *or makif*—an encompassing light.

The unlimited force of Godliness, known as *makif*, is the only thing that can bring physical existence into being from spiritual-

---

5. *Vayikra Rabbah* 30, 12.

ity. Physicality and spirituality are complete opposites, and even the lowest form of spirituality cannot, by its very nature, become physical. Therefore, an unlimited force, one capable of the impossible, is required to bring this about. This force is expressed equally in every created entity.

The limited force, known as *penimi*, is necessary for the existence of a vast number of different entities, each with its own level and its own nature. A particular plant, for instance a palm tree, has a specialized life force giving it its particular identity. It also has the general characteristics of a plant: it grows. When we say that an *or penimi* is revealed within a particular entity, besides saying that it adapts itself to the capacity of that entity, we mean that it can be felt by the entity. For example, a person feels that he is alive. An *or makif*, on the other hand, is hidden when it is expressed. We cannot feel the infinite force that is bringing us into existence at every moment from a spiritual source.

We can understand these two modes of Godly expression further by considering the life force within a human being, which is also subdivided into an "encompassing" force and an "inward" force. The general life force of the body is "encompassing" in the sense that it is found in every part of the body equally. We would not say that the hand is more or less alive than the eye. In contrast, there are various "inward" spiritual powers that are expressed in particular parts of the body. The brain is the "vessel" for the intellect, for instance, the heart is the seat of the emotions, and the eye expresses the power of sight.[6] None of the "inward" powers can be expressed without its particular locus.

---

6. *Derech Mitzvotecha, Mitzvat Binyan Beit Hamikdash*, p. 170.

We can now begin to appreciate the spiritual significance of dwelling in a *sukkah*. We explained earlier that spiritually what is *bakesseh*—hidden—on Rosh Hashanah and Yom Kippur is revealed on Sukkot. This refers particularly to forces of Godliness that are *makifim*, which encompass the various spiritual worlds when Jews dwell in a *sukkah*, just as the *sukkah* encompasses the person in a simple sense. Normally *orot makifim*—encompassing lights—cannot be absorbed inwardly. However, from the standpoint of God's essence there is no distinction between *makif* and *penimi* and even a *makif* light can be absorbed inwardly. When we sit in the *sukkah*, we elicit God's essence, and the encompassing lights become *orot mityashvim* (lights that are absorbed inwardly), something only possible through God's transcendence of all limits.[7]

On Sukkot there is also an elicitation within each Jew of the levels of the soul that are called "encompassing." The Jewish soul, as mentioned earlier, is composed of five levels. The highest levels, which are general and pervasive and not associated with any particular faculty, are called *chayah* and *yechidah*. (*Yechidah* is discussed extensively in the chapter on Yom Kippur.) These encompassing levels are hidden throughout the year, and even when they are revealed to a Jew on Yom Kippur, they are still esoteric in nature and therefore they cannot be internalized. The lower levels, which are *penimi*, are expressed in action, intellect, and emotion, and are associated with garments, which fit closely. The *yechidah* is associated with a house. Just as the structure of a house physically encompasses a person, but at a distance, the *yechidah* is esoteric and beyond comprehension. After the service of self-refinement on Rosh Hashanah and Yom Kippur, when a Jew fi-

---

7. *Sefer Hama'amarim Melukat*, vol. 5, p. 29.

nally reveals the most esoteric level of his soul, the service of Sukkot is to internalize this esoteric force so that it has a permanent and inner influence on his intellect and personality. This is accomplished by dwelling in the *sukkah*. The *sukkah*, like a house, represents the encompassing level of the soul revealed on Yom Kippur, and dwelling in the *sukkah* (dwelling also has the connotation of permanence) gives us the ability to internalize the revelation of the Days of Awe and make it permanent.

Along the same lines, the verses quoted above, containing the basic command for the holiday of Sukkot, state "every native in Israel shall dwell in *sukkot*." The Ba'al Shem Tov states that this verse is actually a promise. Rabbi Shalom Dovber of Lubavitch explains this statement to mean that when a person dwells for seven days in the *sukkah*, he has a promise from God. If he works for seven days with his *nefesh, ruach,* and *neshamah,* the *makifim* levels—which will shine when *Mashiach* comes—will shine now in an inward way.[8] The word for native is *ezrach,* which contains the root "z-r-ch," meaning "to shine." With the added *alef* at the beginning, *ezrach* means "I will shine." Dwelling in the *sukkah* for seven days is thus a continuation of Yom Kippur, when the *yechidah* shines. However, on Sukkot the level of *yechidah* (which is *makif*) has an effect even on the lower levels (*penimim*) of the soul; the *yechidah* shines even in them.[9]

In spiritual service, dwelling in the *sukkah* is "so that you will know" that God "had the Jewish people dwell in *sukkot*." The encompassing levels of the *neshamah* that are elicited on Sukkot should affect the level of the intellect known as *da'at*—the level

---

8. *Keter Shem Tov*, supplements, p. 149.

9. *Sefer Hama'amarim* 5704, "*Besukkot Teishvu,*" p. 32. See also "*Sefer Hama'amarot* 5742, "*Besukkot Teishvu.*"

at which a person senses the relevance of the concept learned to his own existence.

To explain, all Israel are "believers, the children of believers,"[10] for each one has simple faith immediately upon being born, faith totally unclouded by doubt. However, serving God requires effort, so that one's faith will come to involve the intellect. When one believes, one needs to labor so that the intellect will confirm what is believed. The reason is not that one needs to verify that what he believes is correct, for no proof is necessary for faith, which comes from the soul, part of God. Moreover, the soul can be said to "see" Godliness as with spiritual eyes. Nevertheless, if one does not bring the faith into intellect, then a very lofty faculty is not employed in the service of God, and it is as if Godliness is not relevant to the intellect. Since God's unity has to be expressed and appreciated everywhere, if it does not penetrate the intellect, then this circumstance in itself is an obstacle to God's unity. Therefore, there is a mitzvah to "know the God of your father."[11] In mystical terms, faith is "encompassing," beyond the particular faculties of the soul, and when the person brings it into intellect, he brings it into a level that is *penimi*. Afterwards the person will come to a higher level, as he meditates and comes to the conclusion that what he knows is a limitation and that there are higher levels that he cannot comprehend intellectually at all, and for which he needs faith alone.

The concept, then, of the service of Sukkot is to take the lofty but elusive aspects (*makifim*) of faith and internalize them. Therefore the verse "in order that your generations will know" [that God made the Jewish people dwell in *sukkot*]" emphasizes not just the

---

10. *Shabbat* 97a; *Tanchuma*, Exodus 23.
11. I Chronicles 28:9.

sitting in the *sukkah,* but the knowing, that faith should "come down" into knowledge.

THE FOUR SPECIES

The next mitzvah of Sukkot begins on Sukkot morning, when a Jew takes the four species and waves them, drawing them to his heart at the end of each motion.

The accomplishment of dwelling in the *sukkah* and taking the four species, taking the encompassing light and bringing it down to enable it to have an inner effect on the Jewish people, can be illustrated with an analogy. A teacher's understanding of a subject can be totally above the intellectual level of his students. In order to teach them, he has to stop thinking on his own level and find a limited lower level that his students can easily understand. As he condenses his thoughts and limits his intellect, he still remains above his students' understanding. Nevertheless, when he condenses his thought process, and starts teaching the way the student thinks, then he is successful. In the same way, the encompassing light is likened to the teacher's intellect before it becomes condensed, a level that is totally esoteric for the students. Every aspect of the holiday of Sukkot, the revelation of what was elicited on the Days of Awe, corresponds to a stage in the teacher's transmission of the concept and the students' understanding of it. Dwelling in the *sukkah* is that step in which the students fully comprehend the concept intellectually. Taking the four species is the stage in which the intellectual appreciation of the concept actually affects the students' emotions.

On Rosh Hashanah the whole focus of our prayers is to elicit a revelation of God's unity in the world, and this is the idea of the revelation of the encompassing light. The *sukkah* symbolizes that

God's unity transcends all division since it encompasses the various levels of a person (from the head to the feet) equally.[12] The four species continue the theme of revealing God's unity since their uniqueness is that they all possess physical characteristics associated with unity (since they derive from a spiritual source that represents this trait).[13]

The *etrog*, a citrus fruit, is unique in that it requires every season to ripen properly, and it thus demonstrates unity by uniting all the seasons.[14]

The branches of the *lulav*, the palm tree, grow close together, which is also a symbol of unity, and the myrtle branch contains clusters of three leaves, each coming from *one* stem.[15]

Of the willow it is said that "its plants grow with brotherhood."[16] The four species thus represent the unity of God, who is the One true existence.

From one standpoint, the four species represent a lower level of unity than the *sukkah* since the latter reveals a level of Godliness that is above division, as explained above. Despite the dimension of unity in each of the four species, they are nevertheless four separate species that become unified, thereby demonstrating that despite the division that exists in the world, every detail is nevertheless subservient to God's unity, which pervades everything. However, in a sense, the unity represented by the four species is actually loftier than that represented by the *sukkah*.

---

12. The *sukkah* also encompasses all Jews equally, no matter what their spiritual level, as hinted in the Talmud's statement," All Israel is worthy to dwell in one *sukkah*" (*Sukkah* 27b).

13. *Siddur Admor Ha'emtza'i, Sha'ar Halulav* 264d.

14. *Sukkah* 35a.

15. *Sukkah* 32b.

16. *Shabbat* 20a, Rashi.

Normally we think of multiplicity and details as contradictions to God's unity. However, from the standpoint of God's essence, there is no limit to what He can be. Since He is absolutely everything, He can be every detail *as a detail* without contradicting His simplistic unity. This is demonstrated by these four species: although they are details, divine unity shines in them nevertheless.

Our ability to reveal God's oneness in the physical world through our spiritual service is a direct result of Rosh Hashanah and Yom Kippur, when we connect to God's essence, the True Oneness. We are connected to the "One Place" in the physical world, the Holy of Holies, on the "One Day" of the year,[17] Yom Kippur, with the "One Man," the *Kohain Gadol*, and we have returned to the essence of our soul—the *yechidah*—that is united (i.e., made one) with the One God.

THE INCENSE OF YOM KIPPUR AND
THE *SECHACH* OF THE *SUKKAH*

On Rosh Hashanah and Yom Kippur we connect to God's esoteric forces, which (as we have explained in connection with the *yechidah* of the soul) are encompassing. Following that, on Sukkot the *sukkah* represents the encompassing light, and dwelling in the *sukkah* helps us to internalize it. It is interesting to note that in Jewish Mysticism, the smoke and clouds that the *Kohain Gadol* created when he offered the incense in the Holy of Holies becomes the covering of the *sukkah*.[18] This means that what the clouds of glory represent spiritually, the encompassing light, is

---

17. *Menachot* 18a, *Tosafot*.
18. See *Ateret Rosh*, beginning *Sha'ar Yom Hakippurim* 36a.

elicited and drawn forth by the *Kohain Gadol's* burning of the eleven spices, as the Holy of Holies fills up with smoke.

Burning incense subdues the forces of impurity because the cloud of smoke that filled the room surrounding everything in it represents an encompassing light, which is able to elevate these forces of impurity. The encompassing light symbolized by the smoke becomes the spiritual theme of Sukkot, when we internalize this encompassing light. The sounding of the one hundred *shofar* blasts of Rosh Hashanah is also related to the coming of Sukkot, particularly the *sechach*, the covering of the *sukkah*, as indicated by the fact that the word *sechach* has the numerical value of one hundred.[19]

According to *halachah*, the *sechach* must produce more shaded area within the *sukkah* than sunlit area; otherwise the *sukkah* is disqualified. Thus, although the conceptual associations of sun are relevant, those of shade predominate. Just as the holiday of Sukkot is a continuation of the revelation of Yom Kippur, the two aspects of sun and shade are a continuation of the pattern represented by the sacrifices in the Holy Temple—or in contemporary times, by our prayers, which substitute for the sacrifices.

The Torah tells us that animal sacrifices brought to the Holy Temple were to be burned on the altar.[20] The fire represents heat, as does the sun. However, the burning of the incense, causing smoke, which is related to the cloud that protected the Jews for the forty years in the desert, represents shade. On Yom Kippur, although there were animal sacrifices, the essential service of the

---

19. *Pri Eitz Chaim, Sha'ar Hasukkot*, end.

20. Although the animal was consumed by fire which came from heaven, it was a mitzvah for the *Kohein* to kindle a fire on the altar as well.

day is the burning of the incense in the Holy of Holies, and this is revealed on Sukkot, when shade predominates over sun in the covering of the *sukkah*.

The difference between the sacrifices and the incense can be understood by their names in Hebrew. In Hebrew, the word for sacrifice is *karban* (bringing close), meaning bringing one's faculties and senses closer to God. One of the principal concepts of chasidic philosophy is that there are two souls, the Godly soul and the animalistic soul. The Godly soul is mainly concerned with Godliness, as its name indicates, while the animalistic soul is concerned with the self. The Godly soul's mission is to refine the animalistic soul by meditating on matters that it can relate to, for instance that God is the source of all life and a person naturally loves his own life.

The goal and outcome of this service is "closeness" to God, and when a person is merely "close" to God, he still has a sense of individual autonomy and his service is motivated by reason and rationale. This feeling is also related to the heat and warmth of the sacrifices because service motivated by reason is connected to converting the excitement (the "heat") of the animalistic soul into love of God. (The animalistic soul is mainly associated with *middot*—emotion-traits—which are usually characterized as "warm.")

In contrast, the service to God known as *ketoret* is to tie oneself to God and achieve complete unity with Him. The Hebrew word for burning incense is *ketoret*, which can be translated as "tied." Not only is one close to God, but tied, unified with Him.[21] This connection is rooted in the innermost depths of the heart and does not produce external excitement in the person.

---

21. *Torat Shmuel, Yonati* 5640, p. 56.

There is another difference between animal sacrifices and incense. Animal sacrifices were offered in the courtyard of the Holy Temple, outside the actual Temple. The incense was offered inside the Holy Temple. The difference between the outside and the inside corresponds to the two different relationships discussed above that one can have with God. One is an external commitment in which the person retains his sense of autonomy, as if he and God are still two separate entities. However, the service to God with incense, *inside* the Holy Temple, represents the Godly soul's cleaving to God.

There was also a difference between the components of the two types of sacrifices. The animal sacrifices had to be only kosher animals. The eleven spices in the incense included a non-kosher one, myrrh. When a Jew serves God with his external heart, not yet on the level of total unity, he has to be careful, generally, in his service to avoid feelings of self. In contrast, when one serves God with a commitment beyond a feeling of self, the feeling of self is turned into a positive quality. This is why the spices contained the eleven components, one of them from a non-kosher and impure animal. Ten represents spiritual perfection, and ten plus one represents the forces of impurity. The connection between the theme of Yom Kippur and bringing the eleven spices in the Holy of Holies is that since a person reveals his *yechidah* on Yom Kippur, eliciting the encompassing light, even the most negative quality can be transformed into a positive one. In the language of the Talmud, even willful sins can be converted to *mitzvot*.

Since the eleven spices represent impurity, a person's service to God on Yom Kippur, taking the place of the High Priest, has to be beyond limitations in order to "bring down" an infinite light. The love of being "tied" as one with God can transform even impurities into something holy. This leads to the explanation of why the stars must be visible through the *sechach* of the *sukkah*, even though there is supposed to be "more shade than sun."

Chasidic philosophy associates the stars with an even greater light than the sun. While they appear to be small, because they are farther away from the earth than the sun, most stars are actually larger than the sun. Spiritually speaking, the stars represent a higher spiritual "energy" than that of the sun, an infinite (or encompassing) light. On Sukkot we shade the sun, but not so much that we cannot see the stars, thus emphasizing the benefit of starlight over the benefit of sunlight.

THE SEVENTY BULLS

Once the encompassing light permeates the Jew through his intellect and his heart, the next step corresponds to the sacrifice of the seventy bulls, which took place on Sukkot during Temple times.

The number seventy represents the seven emotions of the *kelipah* of *nogah*.[22] This is the source of all the nations of the world. The purpose of the seventy sacrifices is to refine and elevate the sparks and energies found in the nations. This refinement means that it is revealed within the Godly energy that gives life to the seventy nations that their purpose is to serve God. In addition, the seventy sacrifices give the nations sustenance.

---

22. In Jewish mysticism, evil is represented as *klipah*, literally a shell, similar to that covering a fruit. Generally, holiness or goodness is associated with light, and *klipah* is pictured as darkening or covering up the light. *Nogah* means light, and thus *kelipat nogah* is a mixture of good and evil. See *Tanya*, chapter 1.

This is the continuation of the spiritual elicitation of Yom Kippur, when the clouds are created by the incense. The actual spiritual manifestation occurs during the holiday of Sukkot, and therefore the strength of that infinite light serves to purify the source of the nations of the world.

There is an additional reason that the elevation of the nations of the world takes place on Sukkot. Throughout the year a Jew contains a mixture of good and evil, and he is unable to purify the nations of the world until after Yom Kippur, when he rids himself totally of impurity. This takes place in particular after the four days between Yom Kippur and Sukkot, which are spiritually loftier than Yom Kippur.

The seventy bulls are offered as follows: thirteen are offered on the first day, twelve on the second, and so on, decreasing in number until the seventh day, when seven bulls are offered. The decreasing pattern represents the idea of a progressive weakening of the forces of impurity. Beginning with the number thirteen, every entity "on the side of holiness," i.e., in holy part of the spiritual realm, corresponds to a counterpart entity on the "side of impurity." The number thirteen in Kabbalistic terms represents the thirteen attributes of mercy, which are by nature infinite. Therefore, the forgiveness of Yom Kippur stems from the number thirteen, representing infinity. As stated in the Torah, God always answers when we cry out to Him using the thirteen attributes since the infinite power of the thirteen attributes overcomes any unworthiness in the person. However, there are thirteen forces of the "other side." These are manifested when a person becomes involved in the profane to a degree that defies logic, for instance when a person repeats a sin over and over again without feeling that he is doing anything wrong.

On the first day of Sukkot, the thirteen bulls were brought as sacrifices to elevate the thirteen attributes of *kelipah*—to elevate them in the thirteen attributes of mercy. The first day of Sukkot represents the first and most powerful of the seven emotions, *chesed* (kindness), since a strong light is required to elevate a very powerful impure energy. The second day of Sukkot represents the emotion of *gevurah* (strength or severity), which is a step lower than kindness. It is weaker than *chesed* and lacks the ability to counteract the impurity of thirteen. Its level, and the level of the impurity it is able to overcome, is symbolized by the number twelve, thirteen diminished by one. Finally, the seventh day, representing *malchut*, when seven bulls were offered, only has the ability to elevate the impure in the number seven. Decreasing for seven consecutive days to the number seven is thus meant to eliminate the encompassing light of impurity and elevate the seven emotions of the opposite side.

We can also understand an apparent contradiction. On one hand, chasidic philosophy explains that the offering of the seventy bulls throughout the holiday of Sukkot was to give the seventy nations of the world sustenance. On the other hand, the offering of the seventy bulls elevated impurity and made it less powerful.

This can be understood by way of analogy. When a person eats, two things happen: Intellect and understanding and the body in general is strengthened, and the deterioration of the food produces waste. Similarly, on Sukkot two things happen simultaneously. The good of the impurities is elevated, and the negative aspect of the impurities becomes diminished.

On Sukkot, the image of God embracing or hugging specifically refers to embracing from the back, like a person not letting another person go because his love is so strong. If we compare kissing to hugging we see that kissing is more external, and hugging is more intimate and intense. Spiritually, facing another person represents inner feeling and taking delight in God, and embracing from the back is without feeling or enjoyment. Thus, on holidays, when we take delight in the spiritual, we are "facing" God. When we speak of God's embracing us from the back on Sukkot, it means that even when our backs are turned to Him, so to speak, as we are preoccupied with our mundane involvements during the year, we shouldn't depart from Him. Alternatively, the message is that we should always remain on the level associated with "facing" God.

Finally, *Shemini Atzeret* is the delight resulting from the elevation of the source of all the nations. Since everything is absorbed on *Shemini Atzeret*, it is the day to appreciate the spiritual accomplishment of Sukkot.

SIMCHAT BEIT HASHO'EIVAH

Another unique observance that took place on Sukkot in Temple times, and which continues in contemporary times as a celebration, is the drawing of the water for the water libation on the altar. On Sukkot there were, thus, two types of libations, the water libation and the normal wine libation accompanying the sacrifices. The water drawing and the water libation were performed in Temple times with great celebration for seven full days. What is the connection between the water libation and Sukkot? Moreover, the Talmud's[23] statement that one who has not witnessed the celebration of the water drawing has never seen joy in his lifetime also requires explanation.

As explained earlier, the theme of *Shabbat* is delight, and the theme of *Yom Tov* is rejoicing. The nature of delight is almost the complete opposite of the nature of joy, for joy is an internal feel-

---

23. *Sukkah* 51a (*Mishnah*).

ing, while joy is external and readily evident. The more the joy, the more it erupts out. In chasidic terms, *Shabbat* is associated with the attribute of *chachmah* (wisdom), and Yom Tov is associated with *binah* (understanding). The attribute of *chachmah* in a human being is likened to the "flash of light" that brings a new idea or an answer to a question. At that point, there is an inner feeling of delight in perceiving the new concept or idea. However, the idea is not developed yet, and needs to be understood fully by using parables, details, etc. When one finally understands the new concept, the reaction is one of joy rather than delight.

The different reactions result from differing causes. When a new idea enters one's mind, what is appreciated is not the logic of the idea, but rather that it "clicks" and relates to the innermost part of the mind, which is related to the inner part of the soul. The appreciation of the logic of an idea is more external, less connected to the inner dimension of the soul. Therefore, the reaction is also an external one, which is joy. In this light, *Shabbat* is likened to the expression of *chachmah*, and *Yom Tov* to *binah*.

Another difference between *chachmah* and *binah* is that *chachmah* is a sudden flash without self-generated intellectual effort. The essence of *binah*, by contrast, is that the self is engaged; the mind fully comprehends all the stages associated with the working out of the idea. The difference between *chachmah* and *binah*, thus, also parallels the difference between *bitul*—self nullification (associated with *chachmah*)—and *yeshut*—a feeling of self (associated with *binah*). In service to God, *Shabbat* emphasizes *chachmah* (delight) and a feeling of *bitul*, whereas on *Yom Tov*, spiritual service involves increasing understanding of God through meditation so that the joy results from what one understands. This is why there is a biblical commandment to drink wine on *Yom Tov*. Wine is the symbol of understanding a concept whose ramifications have been worked out. Just as wine itself was first a "secret," a substance hidden in the grape, and just as it is only obtained through the squeezing of the grape, something not yet comprehended and fully understood can be cognitively "revealed" through intellectual effort. Another reason why wine physically makes one happy is that it has the potential to bring out the inner joy concealed in a person. This, then, is the meaning of the wine libation: using the attribute of *Binah* to comprehend Godliness.

The water libation on Sukkot represents a different spiritual theme. Water has no taste or color whatsoever, and rather than providing nourishment, it serves to quench thirst or aid digestion. Water symbolizes simplicity—it is something that has no color or form. In the service to God, it is simple acceptance of God as our King. We are His servants based on our pure belief beyond logic of any kind.

The drawing and pouring of the water represents the height of spiritual service, which comes after one understands as much as possible (pouring the wine). The service of water is simple attachment to God beyond reason and rationale, and thus the joy of the water drawing is unlimited, since the joy is not based on inherently limited understanding. The joy engendered the essence of our souls connecting to the essence of God beyond logic has no boundaries whatsoever.

A Jew during *Simchat Beit Hasho'eivah* is like a servant who dances before the King and who feels the joy of serving the master. In II Samuel 12–22, a famous incident occurs in which the Ark of the Covenant is transported into Jerusalem and King David, according to the Torah, "danced with all his might before the Lord." David's complete abandon leads his wife, Michal, to rebuke him for lowering his dignity, but actually his dancing reflected his tremendous self-nullification before God and was a supreme form of spiritual service. This kind of rejoicing is associated with *Simchat Beit Hasho'eivah.*The Rambam comments,

"Everyone who humbles himself and makes himself insignificant [in this kind of rejoicing] is great, honored, and termed one who serves [God] motivated by love."[24]

In summation, *Shabbat* is the service to God in the form of delight and "*bitul*," and *Yom Tov* is the service to God with understanding and comprehension of the greatness of God. The uniqueness of the celebration of joy and *Simchat Beit Hasho'eivah* is the celebration of joy out of pure simple belief in God (joy and *bitul*), resulting from our connection to Him. This is a higher level of *bitul*, a person has so completely nullified his ego that his joy is that of a servant whose whole existence is giving pleasure to his master—joy completely unfettered by the limitations of ego.

---

24. Rambam, *Hilchot Lulav* 8:15.

5

৵৵

Shemini Atzeret and *Simchat Torah:* Dancing with the King

"On the eighth day there will be an *atzeret* for you." (Numbers 29:35)

The word *atzeret* in *Shemini Atzeret* means "holding back," and it is interpreted to mean holding back from doing the labors forbidden on a holiday. This distinguishes *Shemini Atzeret* from all the other holidays, in which the prohibition of doing labor is a function of the holiness of these days, simply called *mikra kodesh* (a holy convocation). On *Shemini Atzeret*, by contrast, the prohibition of labor is a special command, and the day is not called *mikra kodesh* in connection with the prohibition of labor.[1] This raises the question of what exactly is different about the day.

---

1. This term is used in connection to the sacrifices of *Shemini Atzeret* (Leviticus 23:37).

The *Midrash* states that *Shemini Atzeret* can be understood through an analogy about a king who, out of kindness, invites not only friends to a feast, but everyone in the whole country. However, after the party is over, the father (the king) turns to his children and implores them to stay a little longer and refrain from leaving so that they can share the party a little longer with him, and enjoy whatever is left of the food etc.[2]

The meaning of the above is that *Shemini Atzeret* is a continuation of Sukkot: After the great feast of Sukkot, the king asks his children not to depart and to remain another day, i.e., the Jewish people are asked to continue the closeness to God that occurs on a holiday. Therefore, since *Shemini Atzeret* is merely an extension of Sukkot and not essentially a holiday in its own right, it is not called *mikra kodesh*, but simply a day when labor is prohibited.

This is one of the explanations that *Shemini Atzeret* is called, in the language of the Talmud,[3] "a festival in its own right,"[4] meaning a unique festival. We do not refrain from labor because it is a holiday. On the contrary, it is a holiday because it is forbidden to do labor. This means that the *Midrash* in which the king says, "Your departure is difficult for me, stay one more day," implies that the holiday should only be seven days. It is only that when the time arrives "to depart," at the end of the seven days, God says, "You should remain another day so that I can enjoy you." Thus, *Shemini Atzeret* is not a holiday that was established for

---

2. *Bamidbar Rabbah* 29:36.

3. *Sukkah* 47b.

4. This interpretation follows Rashi's interpretation of the plain sense of Numbers 39:35, that *"atzeret"* means *"atzurim"*—"restricted" to do labor. However, see Rashi on the Talmud, *Sukkah* 48a, *Rosh Hashanah* 4b, *Yoma* 3a, *Chagigah* 17a; Ramban, *Sukkah* 37b ff.

some reason intrinsic to the holiday itself; rather it is in the category of an *addition* to Sukkot, one that originated "when the time came to depart." This is why the prohibition of labor of *Shemini Atzeret* is different from that of all the other holidays, when the reason for the prohibition is that it is "a holy convocation." Thus, on *Shemini Atzeret* the Torah does not mention any positive observance, but only uses a negating statement, the prohibition of doing labor. Thus, we are instructed to "withhold" ourselves (to be *atzurim*) from doing labor, for since *Shemini Atzeret* is not a holiday in its own right, the holiness of the day does not make it a holiday with a prohibition of doing labor. On the contrary, the Jewish people fulfill God's request to remain with Him by refraining from doing labor, and this causes the day to have the sanctity of a holiday.[5]

According to chasidic philosophy, *atzeret* also means retaining and absorbing,[6] meaning that everything that was elicited and drawn down on Rosh Hashanah, Yom Kippur, and Sukkot is absorbed permanently, and because of this the holiday is designated as *shemini* (the eighth), indicating that it is a continuation of the seven preceding days. This means that everything that was elicited in a manner of *makif* by dwelling in the *Sukkah* and taking the four species is elicited in a manner that allows it to become incorporated into the person's make-up so that there is no longer any possibility that they will only be transitory. The analogy is given in chasidic philosophy of someone who is thinking about something he does not want to forget, so he dwells on it a bit before going on to the next thought.

---

5. *Likkutei Sichot*, vol. 33, p. 176.

6. *Likkutei Torah*, "Beyom Shemini Atzeret Tihiyeh Lachem," 83a, "*Beyom Shemini*" etc., 84d.

Another nuance of it being called eighth is that the number eight represents infinity. The number seven represents the finite aspect of this world since the normal functioning of nature involves a fixed cycle of seven days. The number eight is one beyond seven, which means it surpasses the finitude of the world. The application of this principle to *Shemini Atzeret* is that in order for the divine "lights" to be "drawn down" and absorbed permanently, an infinite light is necessary.

There is also a teaching of the Maggid of Mezeritch, that *shemini* is an expression of *shomen* (fatness) and *shemen* (oil[7])— for *shomen* indicates the essence of something. According to this teaching, the meaning of *shemini* is that the light of God's essence is elicited and absorbed on *Shemini Atzeret*, and through this absorption, the Jewish people come to resemble the King. According to this, *atzeret* is an expression of "this one will rule (*yatzor*) over My people."[8] Coming to resemble the King means that the Jews are able to "rule over," i.e., have a positive influence on the world around them, rather than being affected by it.

Another implication of the interpretation that *shemini* means essence is that it is the essence of the holidays of the month of *Tishrei*, the time when all the spiritual energies of that month are made permanent. Moreover, all the energies of *Tishrei* are elicited for the whole year, as Rabbi Yosef Yitzchak of Lubavitch writes in the name of Rabbi Schneur Zalman of Liadi, "On *Shemini Atzeret* we receive a granting of ability from above for our spiritual service throughout the year. This is a very great spiritual

---

7. *Likkutei Ma'amorim* of the Maggid of Mezeritch 68b; *Or Torah* (ibid) 95b.

8. I Samuel 9:17. See also Judges 18:7 "[There was no] crown prince (*yoreish etzer*)."

bounty which is elicited through our rejoicing on *Shemini Atzeret* and *Simchat Torah*."[9]

YOUR DEPARTURE IS DIFFICULT

The idea of the Jews remaining another day raises a question: Won't they simply depart the next day? The answer lies in the deeper significance of God's statement "Your departure (*'peridatchem,'* literally 'separation') is difficult for Me." Remaining another day will result in there being no more *pirud*, meaning separation (i.e., disunity among the Jewish people and disunity between the Jewish people and God).

This accords with what we have explored concerning the word *Shemini*, which indicates being above limitations and beyond division. *Shemini Atzeret* thus assures that there won't be any separation, anything that opposes God's infinite unity and the unity between God and the Jewish people, the whole year.

This is why, in particular, the *Midrash* refers to the king's children remaining for *"one* more day." The number one represents

---

9. *Sefer Hama'amarim* 5703. See also *Beyom Shemini Atzeret* 5562, 5678, and 5683. Rabbi Shalom Dovber of Lubavitch notes that the essence of the spiritual revelations of *Tishrei* are revealed in spiritual service throughout the year, enabling a person to accomplish spiritually whatever is relevant to the particular time that he is in. Rabbi Dovber uses the analogy of someone adding water to a concentrate.

This also explains why we say *"Morid hageshem"*—"He causes the rain to fall"—on *Shemini Atzeret*. The basic reason is so that we do not have rain on *Yom Tov*. The deeper reason is that the Torah (and Judaism in general) is called rain (Deuteronomy 32:2). We want the spiritual revelations of *Tishrei* to be elicited throughout the whole year.

God's unity, just as the theme of the parable of the king and his children is the unity and togetherness that they share. This unity is higher than division, so that remaining enables the Jewish people to unify with God for a whole year.

This explains why the expression is "*your* separation is difficult for me," for seemingly it should be, "our separation." However, as far as God is concerned there is ultimately never any separation and He is constantly unified with the Jewish people.

The separation is in the Jewish people themselves, that "you turned your backs to Me and not your faces." This separation between the Jewish people and God comes from the fact that there is *peridatchem* (*your* separation)—disunity among the Jews, one Jew not being unified with his fellow.

In our daily prayers we request "Bless us, our Father, all of us as one." However, when there is lacking "the all of us as one" then there is also lacking the "bless us, our Father," and this is the meaning of the statement, "Let us celebrate together, all of us as one" in reference to *Shemini Atzeret*. For even though Sukkot possesses the service of unity, the concept of the four species— all the categories of the Jewish people are united—nevertheless there is not an essential unity as one entity, since the mitzvah is to take four *separate* categories and unite them.

However, the unity of *Shemini Atzeret* is represented by one bull. This is not the unification of separate entities, but one bull, complete unity as one entity. Therefore, through the one bull, the joining together for one day accomplishes that for the whole year there will be no disunity among Jews, and therefore no disunity between the Jews and God.

In the seven days of Sukkot, the spiritual accomplishments of Rosh Hashanah and Yom Kippur and of the general theme of the ten days of repentance are drawn down (on a level of *makif*, see the chapter on Sukkot) until the perfection of repentance of Yom

Kippur is reached. By drawing down these spiritual matters and absorbing them permanently on *Shemini Atzeret*, on the day of our holiday, a singular expression, the connection and unity of the level of *yechidah* of the soul (see the chapter on Yom Kippur) with the level of God called *Yachid* is revealed (so that it also becomes permanent). The accomplishment of the repentance of Yom Kippur in reaching this level is stressed by the sacrifice of *one* bull, *one* ram.[10]

While it is true, as we have been saying, that on *Shemini Atzeret* the spiritual aspects of Rosh Hashanah and Yom Kippur are also internalized, the holiday should nevertheless still be especially considered a continuation of Sukkot. The reason is that Rosh Hashanah and Yom Kippur in Kabbalah have the theme of "elevation from below upwards," elevating the physical realm and bringing it closer to the spiritual. In kabbalistic terms, starting with Rosh Hashanah and continuing to *Ne'ilah* there is the elevation of the spiritual level of *malchut* higher and higher until the ultimate elevation is reached. In individual spiritual service, a person starts from his lowly state to return to the ultimate closeness to God. In the process he is elevating the energies of the world that are connected to him so that they also become closer to God. Up until *Ne'ilah* a person is asking for a good and blessed year. The response to his request starts on Sukkot, as a spiritual bounty is granted from above. In kabbalistic terms, a result of the elevation of *malchut* is that a new Godly light shines from above to illuminate the world. Since the essential thing is that the world should change and that God should have a dwelling here below, the absorbing alluded to in the name *Shemini Atzeret* especially

---

10. This first paragraph is based on *Sefer Hama'amarim Melukat*, vol. 1, p. 373, sec. 11.

stresses internalizing the inspiration of Sukkot. The holiday's status as a continuation of Sukkot is also another reason that it is called *Shemini*[11] (eighth), indicating that it is a continuation of the seven preceding days.

The theme of absorbing and making permanent all of the spiritual aspects of the holidays of *Tishrei* explains why the celebration of *Simchat Torah*, which acknowledges the fact that the Jews received the second tablets once again, is celebrated in Israel on *Shemini Atzeret* while outside of Israel it is celebrated on the second day, which is merely an extension of *Shemini Atzeret*. The basic explanation for celebrating for two days outside of Israel goes back to the time when the day of *Rosh Chodesh* was determined by the court in Jerusalem based on the testimony of witnesses spotting the new moon. In areas far from Jerusalem there would be doubt as to when to celebrate the holiday, because they could not receive messengers from the court in time, so they would observe the holiday for two days. Chasidic philosophy, however, explains that the deeper reason for celebrating two days is that the spiritual revelation of the festival can be absorbed in one day by those dwelling in the highly spiritual environment of Israel. Outside of Israel, where the physicality of the world is stronger, this revelation must be divided into two parts and absorbed over two successive days.[12]

Chasidic philosophy explains this using the example of an intelligent student who is able to understand something very quickly. A less intelligent student takes a little bit longer to comprehend the same idea. Outside of Israel, the second day of the holiday is no less holy than the first day; the same light is merely spread over two days.

---

11. *Shemini* is also connected to *shuman* and *deshen*.
12. *Derech Mitzvotecha*, p. 198.

We might wonder why we do not celebrate *Simchat Torah* immediately after Yom Kippur, since that is when the second tablets were given. However, since *Shemini Atzeret* means absorbing, and something is much more meaningful to a person and likely to inspire celebration when he thoroughly internalizes it, the time to celebrate the fact that God gave us the Torah once again is not on Yom Kippur, but on *Shemini Atzeret*.

Outside of Israel, there is the advantage of the second day, which is *Simchat Torah*. As we will examine, a rabbinical commandment, or a custom, is even greater than a biblical commandment. Therefore, from a certain perspective, the celebration of the second day outside of Israel has an advantage over the celebration of *Simchat Torah* and *Shemini Atzeret* on the same day in Israel. It should be noted that we see through the generations that *Simchat Torah* outside of Israel is celebrated with more zeal than on *Shemini Atzeret*.

Shemini Atzeret is, as we have said, a continuation of the days preceding it, and it is also a holiday in its own right. We must still reconcile these seemingly contradictory ways of looking at it.

Chasidic philosophy explains the concepts of Sukkot and *Shemini Atzeret*, in terms of the service of God. All Israel are believers, the children of believers, for each one has simple faith immediately upon being born and this faith is simple faith without any doubt whatsoever. However, serving God requires effort, so that one's faith can come to involve the intellect, for when one believes, one needs to labor so that the intellect will confirm what is believed.

The reason is not, God forbid, that one needs to verify that what he believes is correct, for no proof is necessary for his faith, which comes from his soul, part of God. Also, his soul directly experienced Godliness before coming down into a body. Thus, intellectual understanding is not necessary to augment faith, and faith in God, the soul's absolute conviction that stems from direct experience, is stronger than intellectual knowledge to begin with.

Nevertheless, if one does not bring the faith into intellect, then a very lofty faculty remains that is not employed in the service of God, and it is as if Godliness is not relevant to the person, being higher than intellect. Therefore, there is a mitzvah to "know the God of your father." Afterwards, the person will come to a higher level, as he meditates and comes to the conclusion that what he knows is a limitation and that there are higher levels that he cannot comprehend intellectually at all, and for which he needs faith alone.

The concept of the service of Sukkot is to take the lofty but allusive aspects (*makifim*) of faith and internalize them and therefore the mitzvah in order that they will know [that God made the Jewish people dwell in Sukkot] is included in the *mitzvot* of the holiday rather than simply being the reason for the *mitzvot*. This knowing is the knowledge that follows the extending of what faith believes to what intellect understands.

The concept of *Shemini Atzeret* is faith, which must be achieved after the service of comprehending and understanding, and since this comes from spiritual service, it is higher than the *makifim* represented by the *sechach*, the covering, of the *sukkah*. Chasidic philosophy connects this with *Shemini*, coming from the word *shemen* (oil or fat). Just as the fat of something can mean the best, or most essential part (as in the fat of the land), *Shemini Atzeret* expresses the essence of all the holidays of *Tishrei*. The essential theme and goal of spiritual service is to achieve the realization, according to the well-known expression, "the ultimate knowledge is that you do not know."[13] Intellect itself acknowledges that these

---

13. *Techinat Olam* sec. 8, ch. 2; *Ikkarim, ma'amar* 2, end ch. 30; *Shela* 191b.

spiritual matters transcend intellect. Furthermore, the intellect feels a sense of wonder at how these matters transcend intellect, not an actual grasp, but an intellectual appreciation.

We can now understood how *Shemini Atzeret* is a continuation of Sukkot and also a holiday in its right: Spiritually, *Shemini Atzeret* can be said to guard the seven days of Sukkot. In mystical terms it represents a higher level of *makif* than that of Sukkot, so that it serves to unify and protect the spiritual revelations of Sukkot. This is not the main aspect of *Shemini Atzeret*, however, which is the level of ultimate knowledge just discussed.

According to the parable discussed above of the king telling his children to remain one more day, *Shemini Atzeret* is the day that it becomes absolutely clear that God has an infinite relationship with the Jewish people. This begins on Rosh Hashanah when God, once again, chooses the Jewish people and it culminates on *Shemini Atzeret* when the intimate relationship is revealed and takes place. In this way, Rosh Hashanah and *Shemini Atzeret* are bound together. What began on Rosh Hashanah, at the very moment of the *shofar's* sounding, is revealed and appreciated fully on *Shemini Atzeret*. This is why chasidic philosophy analyzes *Shemini Atzeret* as the full revelation and summation of all the holidays of *Tishrei*.

SIMCHAT TORAH

Simchat Torah is celebrated at the completion of the cycle of reading the Torah, when we begin anew to read the Torah. At that time we dance with the Torah and celebrate with unrestrained abandon.

Chasidic philosophy explains that *Simchat Torah* is directly related to Yom Kippur, the anniversary of the giving of the second tablets and the time when God accepts our repentance. The reader will recall an analogy that we used in the Rosh Hashanah chapter to explain the significance of blowing *shofar*. The king sends his son away to learn about the world, and the son becomes alienated from his home, but he finally turns back and reunites with his father. The joy of their reunion is greater than the joy the father originally felt about his son when they lived together in the palace previously. We can continue this analogy and add that in the course of their celebration, the king embraces his son, and finally dances with him. The dancing gets more and more spirited and the father's affection for the son grows to the point where he throws him a most precious gift: the Torah.

The king, as we explained before, is God, and the son is the Jewish people. On Rosh Hashanah, at the sounding of the *shofar*, we repent and achieve a renewed closeness with God. Sukkot is the king's embrace, and on *Simchat Torah*, God's love grows increasingly stronger, and He tells us that He wants to dance with us.

This is why *Simchat Torah* was established to fall immediately after Sukkot (which comes in sequence after Yom Kippur), rather than on *Shavuot*, when the Jewish people received the first tablets. At the giving of the Torah, which is celebrated on *Shavuot*, according to the Talmud,[14] the Jewish people were considered converts, and a convert to Judaism is compared in the Talmud to a newborn baby.[15] He has a completely pure soul, and is thus analogous to a *tzaddik*, one who never sins. On Yom Kippur, in contrast, the Jewish people are likened to *ba'alei teshuvah* (returnees to observance). The *ba'al teshuvah* does *mitzvot* with more

---

14. *Keritot* 9a.
15. *Yevamot* 22a, *Bechorot* 47a.

fervor and excitement than one who never left observance. The reason is that a *ba'al teshuvah* has a past that he must overcome, and his sense of his own sin, his connection to the negative, brings him to realize his great distance from God and to feel a great thirst for Godliness.[16]

GOD'S ESSENCE IN THE TORAH

The emphasis on *Simchat Torah* is not to such a great extent on the fact that we have a Torah that gives us a way of life, or the fact that we have access to God's wisdom. What is crucial is that through the Torah, we can connect with God Himself, for "God wrote Himself into the Torah"[17]—the essence of the Torah is unified with God's essence. Thus, every Jew, no matter what his level of understanding in the Torah, has the same connection to the essence of the Torah since God's essence is equally in every level of the Torah.[18]

This is why the term inheritance is used in connection with the Torah, as in the verse *morashah kehilat Ya'akov*—"an inheritance of the congregation of Yaakov [the Jewish people]."[19] The Torah belongs to every Jew equally, just as the laws of inheri-

---

16. Thus, the Talmud states (*Berachot* 34b, *Sanhedrin* 99a, and *Zohar* I 39a, 129b, III 106b), "in the place [i.e., the spiritual level] a *ba'al teshuvah* stands, even a completely righteous person cannot stand."

17. See chapter on *Shavuot*.

18. The difference between a simple person and Moshe Rabbeinu is: 1) how much that connection is revealed to the person learning and 2) in the advantage of learning that the more one learns the more one is unified (*Tanya* ch. 5) with the Torah.

19. *Devarim* 33:4.

tance apply equally to everyone (even to a one-day-old child, who legally inherits as a mature adult). This is the inner reason why we celebrate with joy and abandon, for the joy results from the realization that we are all equally connected through the Torah to the infinite God.

SIMCHAT TORAH—THE TORAH'S JOY

Chasidic philosophy explains that the name *Simchat Torah* has two explanations. The Jewish people celebrate because they have the Torah, and the Torah itself also celebrates.[20] The Torah celebrates the fact that it receives more holiness through the Jewish people than it has on its own. The source of the Jew's soul is far loftier than the Torah itself, and we also see in the Torah's constant reference to God's speaking to Moses to command the Jewish people that the whole purpose of the Torah is to serve the Jewish people. The Torah is subject to limitation, as we see in the scriptural statement that it is "longer than the Earth . . . and wider than the sea."[21] Even though this statement expresses the greatness of the Torah, it refers to specific, and therefore limited, quantities. The spiritual source of the Jewish people, in contrast, is infinite. Initially the Torah serves as a link between God and the Jewish people. It is able to do this because the Jewish people were created to exist in the physical world as entities apart from God, analogous to children who derive from the essence of their father but who are still separate individuals. The Torah, in con-

---

20. This is also reflected in the phrase "the time of our rejoicing." The plural expression, *"our* rejoicing" refers to the rejoicing of both the Jewish people and the Torah.

21. Job 11:9.

trast, even as it exists on Earth, remains united with God. However, after the stage in which the Jews are connected to God through Torah, the source of the Jew is revealed. At that point, the Jewish people serve as a link between the Torah and God.

After Rosh Hashanah and Yom Kippur the theme of the High Holy days is to bring out the *yechidah* of the Jewish people. On *Shemini Atzeret* and *Simchat Torah*, all is fully internalized, and then the Torah celebrates the soul's contribution to it.

This is the meaning of the two interpretations of the phrase "*Simchat Torah*." The meaning of the statement that the Jewish people rejoice in the Torah is that they rejoice in the fact that they are connected through Torah to God. The Jews' making the Torah rejoice means that once they are connected to God through Torah, their source is revealed, which is higher than the Torah. Then this essential loftiness of the Jewish people is drawn down into the Torah. This quality, which is higher than limitation, is infused into the Torah through the limitless rejoicing of the Jewish people, which in turn makes the Torah "rejoice."

THE GREATNESS OF A CUSTOM

The rejoicing of all holidays is an explicit biblical commandment, and the rejoicing of *Simchat Beit Hasho'eivah* is at least hinted at in the Torah. *Hakafot*, however, are merely a custom. Paradoxically, we find in these three cases that the less of an explicit command there is for the rejoicing, the greater it is, with the joy of *Simchat Beit Hasho'eivah* being greater that that associated with all holidays—and the rejoicing of *Simchat Torah* being the greatest of all. There are two reasons that can be given for this: the first is that when the Jewish people rejoice, even though they are not explicitly commanded, it shows their great devotion to serving God to the extent that they cherish the opportunity in bringing God pleasure. An analogy can be given of three servants, each of whom follows a different approach to serving his master. The first servant does everything he is told, but no more. The second does everything he is told, and in addition, he also performs acts of service that the master only hints that he wants performed. The third, and most devoted servant, performs services for which the master has not even given a hint. The servant's great devotion gives him an insight into what is likely to please the master, and he is able to initiate pleasing acts of service on his own. Similarly, the custom of rejoicing on Simchat Torah derives from the initiative and inner motivation of the Jewish people.

The second reason[22] is that, similar to an explicit biblical command, a custom is also something that God wants carried out. The fact that it is not explicitly stated indicates that it derives from a higher source than an explicit command; it is something too lofty to be spelled out. In other words, there is the revealed will of God, and there is the hidden will of God that is higher than being revealed. These two reasons are actually closely related. Because of the Jewish people's great *devotion* they can reveal even God's desires when they are too lofty to be explicitly stated.

THE MITZVAH OF THE DAY IS *SIMCHAH*

Rabbi Yosef Yitzchak of Lubavitch says of *Simchat Torah* that "The mitzvah of the day is *simchah* (joy)."[23] How does this fit with the

---

22. See *Likkutei Torah*, 86a, 96a.

23. *Sefer Haschot* 5703, p. 8. This is reminiscent of the Talmud's statement, "The mitzvah of the day [of Rosh Hashanah] is blowing the *shofar*" (*Rosh Hashanah* 26b).

idea, as explained above, that *azeret* refers to the prohibition of doing labor so that the holiday has no distinctive positive mitzvah associated with it? If the mitzvah of the day is *simchah*, then is there, seemingly, a positive mitzvah associated with the holiday? We can answer this question as follows:

The obligation to be joyful does not only apply to *Simchat Torah*, but to the whole year, extending to every day and every moment. Service of God is supposed to be with joy, as scripture states, "Serve God with joy."[24] And since a person is obligated to constantly serve God, the obligation to be joyful is a constant one. This being the case, what is the particular obligation to be joyful on *Simchat Torah*?

We must conclude, therefore, that the joy of *Simchat Torah* is entirely different than that associated with our divine service throughout the year. The *simchah* of the whole year is connected with specific matters—the joy stemming from doing a mitzvah or from learning Torah. However, the *simchah* of *Simchat Torah* is not connected to any specific matter, or even learning Torah, which is considered the equivalent of all the *mitzvot*. Rather, this joy is *simchah atzmit* (essential *simchah*). The essence of a Jew's soul is united with the essence of God, and "*simchah atzmit*" is the joy that expresses this unity. This answers our question as to why we can say that *Shemini Atzeret* does not possess any distincitive positive mitzvah. The answer is that this kind of *simchah* is higher than a mitzvah.

This special quality of the *simchah* on *Simchat Torah* also explains why we say that it is necessary to draw on the joy of *Simchat Torah* and extend it into the whole year, even though there is a command in any event to be joyful in our year-round service. This

---

24. Psalms 100:2.

essential simchah should also be part of the joy of any normal spiritual service throughout the year.

HAKAFOT

This special quality of the joy of *Simchat Torah* is expressed in the custom of *hakafot*. Performing *hakafot* involves "circling the reading table seven times with the Torah scrolls in great jubilation, dancing before them, exulting, and making processions with them in great joy."[25] The *simchah*, in other words, is not connected to learning and intellectual understanding of the Torah; it consists completely of celebrating and dancing. During the *hakafot*, not only are we uninvolved in learning and intellectual understanding, there is *no possibility* of being involved in learning the Torah since we are holding the Torah scrolls wrapped in their mantles.

On the surface, this is a puzzling custom. It is obligatory to learn the whole year round, as scripture states, "You shall study [the Torah] day and night."[26] If this is true concerning the whole year, then it certainly must be true on *Simchat Torah*, when we celebrate the completion of the Torah-reading cycle—this is certainly a time in which it is fitting to learn Torah.

Thus, it makes sense to think that we would take the Torah scrolls from the Ark and then open them up in order to read from them. What we do instead is to leave them wrapped up in their covers, a state in which it is impossible to read them, and *dance* with them!

---

25. *Siddur Admor Ha'emtza'i*, *"Seder Hakafot* for *Simchat Torah."*
26. Joshua 1:8.

We can add another point: Besides the greatness of learning Torah (at any time of the year, and especially, one would think, on *Simchat Torah*), there is also the need to be careful to guard the honor of a Torah scroll—it is well-known to be no trifling matter to take a Torah scroll out of the ark for no reason. The gravity of doing this is so great, in fact, that even when we merely open up the ark to take out the Torah, we say "Ascend O God to Your resting place, You and the Ark of Your strength."[27] In other words, the Holy Ark is also to arise to its resting place, along with God, and how much more so the Torah scroll itself.

Nevertheless, we take out *all* the Torah scrolls (not just one) from the Ark and carry them from place to place. And we do not do this to read from them (for one scroll would suffice for this), but to *dance* with them around the reading desk. And this is how the custom of *hakafot* is performed, not reading the Torah, but dancing with the Torah scroll![28]

We can conclude from this that the joy of *Simchat Torah* is not tied to any particular mitzvah, or even "*Talmud Torah* [which is] equivalent to them all."[29] Rather, it is *simchah atzmit* that is expressed—not in understanding or comprehension or something similar—but in dancing, something extremely simple!

Therefore, we find that the joy of *Simchat Torah* is equal for all Jews, whether Torah Scholars or simple people. This is in contrast to *Simchat Beit Hasho'eivah*, in which, as mentioned in the last chapter, the prominent people would dance in the days of the Temple while ordinary people would watch, and thus there

---

27. Psalms 132:8.

28. There is a Torah reading on *Simchat Torah*, but this is an observance that is separate and apart from *hakafot*.

29. Liturgy, Morning Blessings.

are distinctions among different levels. On *Simchat Torah* the rejoicing is not connected to the appreciation of the intellectual beauty of Torah, which would produce different levels of joy for different people, but rather joy connected to the essential existence of a Jew. In this respect, all Jews are equal without distinctions.

We carry the Torah in a circle using our feet. The head is used for Torah study, whereas *Simchat Torah* is not so much celebrated by the study of Torah, but with our legs and dancing with the Torah.[30] This demonstrates that *Simchat Torah* emphasizes the essence of God in the Torah. The legs and the head are equal to God's essence since from an infinite perspective everything is equal, just as the numbers one and a million can be considered equally close to infinity.

Similarly, we find in the letters of the Torah that each letter represents a Jewish soul, and every letter in the Torah is equally important.[31] If any letter is found missing, the whole Torah is invalid, again indicating that the essence of the Torah is equal for everyone alike. This is a direct result of the spiritual events of Rosh Hashanah, when God chooses the Jewish people. Since this choice is not based on their merits or level, all are chosen equally.

Dancing with the Torah also emphasizes the greatness of physical action. The holiday expresses, as we have been saying, the essential joy of the Jewish people and God—the essence of God

---

30. The feet represent acceptance of the heavenly yoke, which is not only the foundation of our spiritual service, but something that is supposed to have an effect on our learning of Torah, i.e., that during the learning we feel that it is God's Torah. The dancing on *Simchat Torah* helps us achieve this for the whole year (*Likkutei Sichot*, vol. 4, p. 1167).

31. The name "Yisrael" can be read as an acronym for "there are 600,000 letters in the Torah."

and the essence of the Jewish people are united through the Torah. As lofty as the essence of the Torah is spiritually, the ultimate intention of the Torah is to physically transform the world. Therefore the holiday is celebrated by the dancing of the legs, physical action, rather than by intellectual appreciation. Chasidic philosophy comments that it is as if we become the legs of the Torah. Just as the legs are required to carry a person from place to place so that the directives of the head can be carried out, we are the means for the realization of God's will contained in the Torah.

We perform *hakafot* three times, on the night and day of Simchat Torah and on the night of *Shemini Atzeret*. It is a principle in Jewish law that anything performed three times establishes a precedent. Therefore, the *hakafot* make the joy of *Simchat Torah* permanent, allowing us to draw upon it the whole *year*.

We can now add a dimension to our understanding of the statement that on *Simchat Torah*, "the mitzvah of the day is *simchah*." There is a key distinction between rejoicing on *Simchat Torah* and other acts of spiritual service that are done on *Simchat Torah*, such as the recitation of *Shema*. This is similar to the distinction just described between the essential joy of *Simchat Torah* and the joy of doing a specific mitzvah during the year. Whereas the recitation of *Shema* on *Simchat Torah*, for instance, is an individual act of service that must be done on *Simchat Torah* as on all other days of the year, rejoicing expresses the essence of *Simchat Torah*.

6

ب

Chanukah: Transforming the Darkness

"A mitzvah is a candle and the Torah is light." (Proverbs 6:23)

The holiday of *Chanukah* seems to commemorate two different miracles. The first was the miraculous victory of the Jews, led by Matityahu and Yochannan the *Kohain Gadol* (the High Priest), over the Syrian Greeks in the year 138 BCE. The second miracle was the discovery of the intact jar of pure olive oil with the *Kohain Gadol*'s seal still on it. The finding of the jar was a miracle in itself, and moreover the oil, which was only sufficient to light the menorah for one day, miraculously lasted for eight days. The military victory took place on the 24th of *Kislev*,[1] while the miracle

---

1. This is the opinion of the *Me'iri* (*Shabbat* 21a). This is the opinion followed in most discussions of this topic in chasidic philosophy. However, according to the opinion of the Rambam (*Hilchot Chanukah* 3:2),

of the oil occurred on the twenty fifth. We begin the holiday of *Chanukah* on the twenty fifth and the establishment of lighting the menorah as the central observance of *Chanukah* also seems to emphasize the miracle of the oil. This emphasis raises an obvious question: Wouldn't it be more appropriate for our celebration to emphasize the military victory and the survival of the Jewish people? The oil miracle seems secondary to the victory, and it would not have been possible had the Jews not been victorious.

CHANUKAH AND *PURIM*

Chasidic philosophy explores this question by comparing *Chanukah* to *Purim*. In the events celebrated on *Purim*, Haman's decree was to annihilate the Jewish people, not because he opposed the Jewish religion per se, but because he hated the very existence of the Jew.[2] By contrast, in the events of *Chanukah*, the Greek Syrian objective was to destroy the Jewish religion. Our rabbis[3] state that the Greeks informed the Jews that if they would "inscribe on the horn of an ox that you have no part in the God of Israel" (i.e., totally repudiate Judaism), they could avoid war.[4]

---

the victory in the war was on the twenty fifth of *Kislev*. See *Ma'amorei Admor Hazakein* 5563, p. 57, *Sha'arei Orah, ma'amar* beginning "*Bechafhei Kislev*," *Derech Mitzvotecha. "Mitzvat Neir Chanukah." See also Likkutei Torah, Tzav*, 16, *Torah Or*, end *Parshat Vayeishev*.

2. Even though they would not have been killed had they repudiated their religion, this was only to escape the decree forcing them to convert. The main decree, however, concerned their very existence. See *Levush, Orach Chayim*, sec. 670.

3. *Bereishit Rabbah* 2,4; see *Torah Or, Vayeishev* 30a.

4. *Talmud Yerushalmi, Chagigah* 2:2.

We see from this that the victory of *Chanukah* is the triumph of the Jewish religion, whereas that of *Purim* is the survival of the Jewish people.

The manner in which we celebrate corresponds to the unique miracles of each holiday. *Purim*, the victory of the physical survival of Jewish people, is celebrated by festivities that relate to the body, such as having a festive meal, sending gifts of food to friends, giving charity to the poor.[5] *Chanukah*, the triumph of the Jewish religion, is celebrated by lighting the menorah, whose symbolism is spiritual,[6] and there is evidently no obligation to have a festive meal.[7]

---

5. Esther 19:22.

6. A scriptural verse (Proverbs 6:23) indicates that the menorah symbolizes religion: "For a mitzvah is a lamp and the Torah light." Chasidic philosophy (*Sefer Hama'amraim* 5643, "*Tanu Rabbanim, Ner Chanukah*") elaborates that either the wick or the vessel symbolize *mitzvot*, a physical means through which a person draws down "light," the divine will embodied in the *mitzvot* (*Sefer Hama'amarim* 5679, "*Ner Chanukah*").

The metaphor of light is often used when referring to spiritual subjects, since light is distinguished from other created entities. Even though it is also created, it does not have the quality of materiality as much as the rest of the world. See *Shomer Emunim, Vikkuach Sheini*, "*Ha'amnam*." See also *Magen David* of the *Ridbaz*, and *Sefer Hama'amarim* 5708, "*Ki Menase*": "Every spiritual existence is light." The above explains the saying of our sages (*Shabbat* 22b) in connection with the lights of the menorah: "[The fact that the western light is kindled at all times] is a testimony to mankind that the divine presence dwells among the Jews."

At first glance, it is not clear how the western light was different from the other ten miracles that were performed for our ancestors in the Temple (*Avot* 5:5, *Yoma* 21a) so that this specific miracle testified concerning the Divine. On the contrary, the menorah seems the least well-suited of the miracles for this purpose since it was located in the sanctuary, a place that almost no one was allowed to enter. And on the other hand, some of the ten miracles took place in the courtyard of the Temple,

JUDAISM AND HELLENISM

If the war of *Chanukah* mainly concerned religion, we might wonder, what was it about the Jewish religion that the Greeks couldn't tolerate? The Greeks were highly cultured and renowned for their great philosophers. In the days of the Maccabees, the prevailing Hellenistic culture was atheistic, exclusively stressing logic and rationale; anything that was beyond the realm of reason was unacceptable. Thus, they had a high degree of respect for the Torah as a remarkable work of culture and they held the Jews in esteem for possessing the intellectual capacity to comprehend something so profound and clever,[8] but they vigorously objected to any notion of the divine nature of Torah. The Jewish attitude, in contrast, is that every word of Torah and every detail of a commandment is Godly.[9] Jews study Torah cognizant of its divinity, and to this the Greeks strenuously objected.

---

and a few outside the courtyard, and in a manner that they were more publicly known.

According to the above, however, it is clear that light, being more intrinsically spiritual, more strongly indicates the Divine Presence.

7. See *Shulchan Aruch, Orach Chayim* 670:2. The Rambam also does not mention an obligation to have a meal, and see the Bach and the Taz. The Ramah writes that there is a certain mitzvah to have festive meals on *Chanukah* and he cites the Maharal of Prague, who writes, "They established feasts and rejoicing [on *Chanukah*]."

8. *Sefer Ham'amarim Yiddish, Ma'amar* 44.

9. *Shabbat* 105a explains the first word of the Ten Commandments, *Anochi* (I), as an acronym for "*Ana nafshi ketavit yehavit*"—"I myself wrote and gave (i.e., "I wrote myself into the Torah")." See *Tanya*, ch. 47: "It is as if He gave us Himself, so to speak." Moreover, the *mitzvot* are the divine will, which is united with His essence; see *Likkutei Torah, Shelach*, 48d; *Or HaTorah, Yitro*, p. 811b.

Similarly, the Greeks did not object to the actual practicing of the *mitzvot*, as long as they were observed for their civilizing value, and not with the approach that they are the will of the infinite God. According to the Jewish attitude, the *mitzvot* are not only beyond the scope of human intellect, but beyond the realm of intellect altogether.

The liturgy of *Chanukah* states that the Greeks wanted the Jews to forget "*Your* Torah and violate the decrees of *Your* will," not the laws themselves, but the Godly aspect. Thus, the main set of laws that the Greeks opposed were the ones called *chukim*, that have no logical explanation. These include the laws of ritual purity and impurity, the prohibition of mixing meat and dairy together, the prohibition of wearing a garment made of a combination of wool and linen, etc. The Greeks wanted these particular laws done away with,[10] and chasidic philosophy explains that this is why the Greeks defiled the oil: in order to nullify the super-rational concept of purity and impurity.

Although the Greeks defiled all the utensils in the Holy Temple, the liturgy only mentions that "when the Greeks entered into the Holy Temple, they defiled all the oils of the Temple." This confirms that the Greeks put special emphasis on defiling the oil. It is also significant that the Greeks *defiled* the oil, rather than disposing of it. The key concept here is what oil symbolizes. Oil is compared to intellect[11]; just as oil always rises to the top when

10. See *Sefer Hama'amarim* 5701 and 5704. This is mentioned in many other sources as well.

11. See *Menachot* 5b, *Zohar II* 94b. See also *Oheiv Yisrael, Chanukah,* Rabbi Yehoshua Heschel of Apt. See also *Degel Machaneh Ephraim, Parshat Mikkeitz,* by Rabbi Moshe Chaim Ephraim, grandson of the Ba'al Shem Tov: The name "Maccabee" comes from the fact that the Maccabees would say the verse "*Mi chamochah be'eilim Hashem, mi chamochah*

mixed with another liquid, intellect is unique in that it can be objective by removing itself from emotions and rising above them.[12] The Greek's goal was to attack the Jewish thought-process by contaminating their intellect and ultimately causing the Jews to think like them. The contaminated intellect of the Greeks for the most part prevailed; indeed they succeeded in "defiling the oil"—many Jews became Hellenists, assimilating into Greek culture.

Nevertheless, the Jew possesses something far deeper than intellect and indeed totally beyond it, the essence of his soul, known as the *yechidah*. This is symbolized by the intact jar of pure olive oil sealed by the High Priest. On the level of *yechidah* a Jew is always united with the essence of the Infinite God and nothing can interfere with this connection. When the Hasmoneans realized that the Greeks were seeking to destroy their attachment to God, they awakened this part of their soul and exhibited self-sacrifice to preserve the essence of their religion. Although the odds were against them—they were a small minority even among

---

nedar bekodesh"—"Who is like You among the supernal beings, O God, who is like You resplendant in holiness" (Exodus 15:11)—while fighting. The end of the verse, *Mi chamochah nedar bakodesh* is connected to oil, which has a direct connection to the word *kodesh*, as in the scriptural phrasing *shemen mishchat kodesh*—holy annointing oil (Exodus 30:25). Moreover, the word *kodesh* is connected to *chachmah* (wisdom), corresponding to what we point out above that oil represents intellect. Thus, the miracle of *Chanukah* reflected the Maccabees's famous battle cry and prayer in praise of God, since the miracle involved oil, which is connected to *chachmah*.

12. Emotions and the feeling of self are inseparable. Only intellect can rise above emotion and achieve an understanding which can even contrary to what emotions believe. The intellect, ultimately, is able to change and control the emotions.

their fellow Jews, let alone compared to the mighty Greek forces—they went forth to meet the enemy, even though logically it was inconceivable that they would win. Their self-sacrifice, which stems from the level of *yechidah*, elicited from God supernatural[13] powers that made them victorious. Since, spiritually speaking, the Jews aroused their *yechidah*—their "intact jar of pure olive oil sealed by the High Priest"—there was a corresponding physical manifestation in their discovery of the intact jar of oil sealed by the High Priest[14] in the Holy Temple.

THE MIRACLE OF THE OIL

It is significant that the oil lasted specifically eight days. There is a direct link between the self sacrifice of the Jews and the number eight, which represents infinity. As mentioned in previous chapters, the physical is a manifestation of the spiritual. The week has seven days because God has seven emotional attributes, each of which was dominant on one of the seven days of creation. The number seven represents the finite aspect of this world since the

---

13. That is, a small band of soldiers was able to defeat a great army.

14. It is written, "with the seal of the High Priest" even though in order to be pure it is sufficient to have the seal of someone who is expert in the laws of ritual purity. The concept of it being sealed with the seal of the High Priest can be understood according to what the High Priest represents spiritually, as indicated by a scriptural verse referring to Aaron the High Priest as "holy of holies" (I Chronicles 23:13). Chasidic philosophy explains (*Sefer Hasichot* 5750, vol. 1, *Vayeishev*) that the High Priest represents the highest level of self-nullification to Godliness reaching the level of self-sacrifice that transcends reason. See also *Sefer Hama'amarim* 5736, "*Be chaf-hei beKislev*" and *Sha'arei Orah*, "*Ketiv, Ki Atah neri*," ch. 7.

normal functioning of nature involves a fixed cycle of seven days. The number eight is one beyond seven, which means it surpasses the finitude of the world.[15] We find many examples where the number eight represents infinity, e.g., circumcision on the eighth day, representing the infinite bond that is established between the child and God, and the eight-stringed harp that the Talmud mentions will be played when *Mashiach* comes, the time in which God's Infinite light will be revealed.[16]

Since the miracle of the oil occurred in connection with the lighting of the menorah in the Holy Temple, one would expect that except for the addition of an eighth candle, the laws and customs pertaining to the *Chanukah* menorah would be the same as those pertaining to the menorah in the Holy Temple. There are, however, a great many differences between them, and this requires explanation. Ultimately, we shall see that the details of the mitzvah of the *Chanukah* menorah all derive from one central spiritual idea, distinguishing it from the one in the Temple.

THE *CHANUKAH* MENORAH AND THE MENORAH IN THE TEMPLE

The differences between the laws of the two menorahs are in the following respects:

1. *In their number:* The menorah in the sanctuary had seven lights while the *Chanukah* menorah has eight. As explained

---

15. *Teshuvat Rashba*, vol. 1, sec. 9.

16. *Arachin* 13b. The *kinor* (harp) that was played in the Temple was of seven strings and that of the days of *Mashiach* will be of eight strings.

above, the duration of the miracle demonstrates in itself that the *Chanukah* menorah is connected to the number eight, unlike the one in the Holy Temple.

2. *In the time they were lit:* In the Holy Temple the menorah was kindled before sundown, while the *Chanukah* menorah must be lit from sundown on.

3. *In their placement:* In the Holy Temple the menorah was placed within the sanctuary whereas the *Chanukah* menorah is placed by the door on the outside.[17] In addition the menorah was positioned on the right hand side[18] in the Holy Temple unlike the *Chanukah* menorah, which is placed on the left hand side of the door post.

Generally, the spiritual concept of the *Chanukah* menorah is to illuminate the spiritual darkness of exile. As mentioned above, the Greeks had managed to penetrate as far as the Holy Temple, a place forbidden even to an Israelite who doesn't belong to the family of *Kohanim* or the tribe of Levites. This entry into the sanctuary and defiling of the oils added powers to the forces of impurity, producing extensive spiritual darkness. When the Jews rallied around the Hasmonean leadership and defeated the Greeks, the lights of *Chanukah* were established in order to illuminate and rectify the Hellenistic spiritual darkness.

---

17. In the language of the Talmud, "At the door of the house to the outside."

18. The menorah is usually spoken of as being in the south. Since the south is associated with hot climates, it is associated with the sun (a luminary) and therefore revelation, which in Jewish mysticism is associated with the "right side." In the same way, the north is cold and associated with the left (*Sefer Hama'amarim* 5643, "*Tanu Rabbanim, Ner Chanukah*").

With the above explanation of the spiritual concept of the menorah, we can grasp the significance of the details of lighting the menorah. The *Chanukah* menorah is lit specifically from sundown when it is dark, symbolizing the concept of illuminating the spiritual darkness. For the same reason the *Chanukah* menorah is supposed to be lit on the left side of the door post. Right symbolizes God's state of complete revelation, in which His presence is felt, enabling us to feel a sense of closeness to Him. Conversely, the left symbolizes withholding Godliness through concealment, which makes us feel distanced from God. Intense concealment ultimately causes impurity and spiritual darkness to be stronger. The goal of the menorah, particularly through its placement on the left, is to overpower and transform the "left" (with its accompanying spiritual darkness) by means of its great light. It is also lit on the "outside," which is the public domain. The public domain (literally "domain of the many") implies a place of plurality, one where multiplicity is felt. Spiritually speaking, plurality implies denial of God's unity since in plurality His presence is concealed and the notion of "other existences" can therefore be conceived. In contrast, the term for the private domain ("domain of the individual") implies unity, symbolizing a place of divine unity, in which only God's presence is felt.[19] Here again, the purpose of the menorah is to illuminate even the darkness associated with the "public domain," the forces opposing God's unity. Only an Infinite light can penetrate such spiritual darkness, and indeed the *Chanukah* menorah's light is infinite. This infinity is exhibited through its link to the number eight, which symbolizes infinity, as mentioned previously. Besides the lamps being eight in number, lighting the *Chanukah* menorah is observed for eight days.

---

19. See chapter on *Shabbat*.

Chanukah's infinite revelation (or light) was elicited through the self-sacrifice of Mattityahu and his sons, who led the Hasmoneans in battle against the Greeks. The great spiritual darkness experienced in that time evoked in them the power of self-sacrifice, which stems from the *yechidah*, the part of the soul that is infinite. Their spiritual service of self-sacrifice elicited a revelation of God's essence, which is infinite. Through this infinite revelation, they were able to illuminate the spiritual darkness.

All the above is in direct contrast to the purpose and effect of the menorah in the Temple. Unlike the *Chanukah* menorah, the Temple menorah didn't directly oppose spiritual darkness; rather its function was to increase spiritual light. The revelations experienced in the Holy Temple were not elicited via self-sacrifice; therefore, they were finite, symbolized by the *seven* lamps, and incapable of transforming and elevating, what only an infinite revelation (light) can accomplish. We can now understand why the Holy Temple's menorah was placed *within* the sanctuary, on the *right* side (the south) and lit *before sundown*. All these aspects point to the Holy Temple's function of increasing the spiritual light but not confronting the "public domain," the "darkness" associated with the left.

Besides the spiritual concept of *Chanukah*, namely, illuminating the darkness, there are two points that require further elaboration and explanation:

Firstly, as we noted, the menorah must be lit from sundown on so that it serves to illuminate the darkness; however, why must the mitzvah commence once it is dark? Wouldn't the same objective be met if the menorah was lit during the day, providing it would last long enough to burn into the night? Secondly, we have explained that the menorah is to be placed on the outside: If the menorah's infinite light is so powerful, would it not in any case "reach the outside"? Why must we so place it to begin with?

To understand these two significant aspects of the mitzvah of the menorah lighting, we must take a look at how God expresses His power of Infinity. There are primarily three levels of God's Infinity, each level being very unique and distinguished from the other. On the first level, God influences everything through a manner of overpowering. This infinite level can reach all the way to the lowest level in our physical world since nothing can limit it. It can defy nature, as in the case of a supernatural miracle, in which the limitations of nature are nullified.

The second level is a higher expression of God's Infinity. On this level God influences everything in a manner that even the lowest levels are not only not negated but influenced to cooperate with the Infinite power. Here the finite nature of the world works hand in hand with Infinity, as in the story of *Purim*, which involves no violations of the laws of nature. These two levels have one aspect in common, they both recognize the existence of many different spiritual levels (that the Infinite power effects) that are considered "higher" or "lower" based on the extent of Godly revelation experienced at that level.

The third level is not an expression of God's infinity, but His very essence. Here the definition of Infinite is not that He is limitless but rather that He is everything.[20] The true existence of everything is the essence of God Himself. Every level, creation, etc. is God Himself. His existence, unlike anything we as finite entities can comprehend, can consist of opposites at the same time. He can be physical, spiritual, finite, infinite, etc.

Taking this a step further, even "opposing forces" otherwise known as "spiritual darkness," are really God Himself. In this respect there is no distinction of levels; we are dealing with God

---

20. It is relevant to note here that oil is associated with essence.

Himself, not expressions or revelations where His presence is felt
to a greater or lesser degree. Spiritual darkness or spiritual light are
equally the essence of God. Our prophets predict that in the ultimate redemption, not only will "spiritual darkness" cease to be an
opposing force that interferes, but it, too, will shine, meaning it will
be apparent that darkness itself is really the essence of God.

The *Chanukah* menorah's light is meant to express the above
concept. In this sense, illuminating the darkness means to reveal
how the spiritual darkness is really the essence of God (as is spiritual light). The emphasis is exclusively directed towards transforming the spiritual darkness so that it shines and radiates God's
essence. When we light the menorah we demonstrate this: We
don't light until it is "dark" and we position the menorah so that it
is directed towards the outside. If we were to light the *Chanukah*
menorah indoors and during the day so that the light extended
into the night, or reached out to the outside, the implication spiritually would be that there is an infinite light extending into the
darkness to influence it through weakening it, but still not transforming it. The *Chanukah* menorah's light, however, shows us that
there is no difference between the spiritual light and spiritual
darkness by revealing the essence of God in the darkness.

"UNTIL THE STEPS OF
THE TARMODITES CEASE"

The Talmud designates the time for lighting in an unusual way:
"From when the sun goes down until the steps (lit. Feet) of the
nation of Tarmodites cease."[21] The Tarmodites were a specific

---

21. *Shabbat* 21b.

group of people that lived in certain areas. They used to appear at sundown only for a half an hour to sell lighting material, i.e., matches, which was their way of making a living. Why does the Talmud choose the Tarmodites to set the menorah lighting time? Wouldn't it be more appropriate to set the time with reference to a universally recognized standard and merely say that from sunset the menorah should be lit for at least half an hour?

Chasidic philosophy offers an explanation by examining the precise wording: The word *Tarmoda'i* (Tarmodites) contains the same letters as the root of the word *meridah*, which means "rebellion." From here it is learned that the Tarmodites symbolized rebellion against the Kingship of Heaven. The menorah is thus lit so that there is not even a trace of the "feet"[22] of rebellion.

Chasidic philosophy goes on to elaborate what the Talmud alludes to with the word cease (*kaliyah*). *Kaliyah* means ceases, but it is also related to the word *kilayon*, which means expiring (as in *kelot hanefesh*, the expiring of the soul as it strives to be united with God). With this additional interpretation we see the purpose of the menorah emphasized. Besides eliminating even a trace of the "feet of rebellion," the *Chanukah* light transforms the "rebellion" so that even the formerly rebellious experience *kaliyah—kelot hanefesh*—expiring and becoming unified with God. This is yet another example of how the menorah illuminates the spiritual darkness and transforms it into light through the infinite revelation of the *Chanukah* illumination.

The chasidic master, Rabbi Yisrael of Rushin,[23] writes that on *Chanukah* a person can influence whether he will have a good year more than on any other holiday. On all other holidays there

---

22. The lowest level.
23. *Orot Yisrael, Chanukah*, p. 245.

is, to use chasidic terminology, an "awakening from below," a spiritual initiation on the part of the Jewish people, and that leads to an "awakening above," a spiritual arousal or evocation on God's part. On *Chanukah* the awakening, or initiation, comes from above first.

This can be understood with the following analogy: When a person comes before a king in his palace to ask him something, the king is exacting concerning whether he is worthy that his wish should be fulfilled. However, when the king is traveling, then even if someone really not worthy makes a request, the king is not exacting. In the verse *"Neir mitzvah veTorah or"*—"A mitzvah is a candle and the Torah is light" (Proverbs 6:23)—*Chanukah* corresponds to the statement *neir mitzvah* and *Yom Tov* to the statement *Torah or*. Therefore on *Chanukah* a person can be helped even if he is not worthy in the merit of performing a mitzvah and because of God's mercy. *Yom Tov*, however, is called *Torah or*, and therefore Hashem conducts Himself according to the Torah, i.e., more strictly.

Purim:
The Advantage of Exile

"And the Jews undertook to do that which they had begun." (Esther 9:23)

The holiday of *Purim* commemorates the defeat of Haman's evil decree to destroy the Jewish people when they were both in exile and under Persian rule. According to our Sages, when the Jews refused to save themselves by submitting to Haman's demand that they reject Judaism, they confirmed their initial acceptance of the Torah at Sinai, which was provisional until then. Each Jew was given a full year to consider and decide, and as Rabbi Schneur Zalman of Liadi writes, "Besides the fact that in practice not one Jew agreed to reject the Torah, not one even considered it for a moment." This explains the expression of our Sages "They accepted what they had accepted before."[1]

---

1. *Shabbat* 88a commenting on Esther 9:27.

HE HELD THE MOUNTAIN OVER THEM

Long before *Purim*, at Sinai, each Jew accepted the Torah and proclaimed *"na'aseh venishma."*[2] However, the Talmud seems to indicate that God subjected the Jews to a threat if they did not accept: "He held the mountain over them like a barrel, and said 'If you accept the Torah, it is well, if not this will be your grave.'"[3] Rabbi Schneur Zalman of Liadi explains that spiritually this means that God exhibited such a great love for the Jewish people that it was like being embraced by God from all sides. The experience was so overwhelming that the Jews were as compelled to accept as they would have been under a dire threat.[4] The Talmud even comments that the Jews could claim later that they only accepted the Torah under duress if they violated it.[5]

In contrast, the events of *Purim* occurred during a time of exile, a time devoid of divine revelation, and nevertheless all the Jews stood firm in their self-sacrifice in order to sanctify God's name. Chasidic philosophy explains that sometimes spiritual interactions between God and human beings are initiated by God and sometimes by human beings. In the events of *Purim* everything was in the mode of human initiation, and the Jews' original acceptance of the Torah was confirmed and clarified. Only then was it clear that the Jews at Sinai acted of their own volition, and not simply due to the great revelation.

---

2. "We will do and we will understand." By mentioning that they would obey the commandments before mentioning understanding them, the Jews demonstrated an unconditional willingness to accept the commandments.

3. *Shabbat* 88a.

4. *Torah Or, Megillat Ester*, pp. 98–99.

5. *Shabbat* ibid.

To consider this more deeply, we should recall that the Torah was given so that there should be a fusion of the physical and the spiritual, the ultimate goal of God's creation of the universe. This fusion is possible only through the revelation of God's essence, which is able to join opposites. However, the intention is that human beings should elicit the revelation of Divinity through *their own* labor, and this is the unique accomplishment of *Purim*. This joining of the upper realms and the lower realms, the spiritual and the physical, accomplishes the goal of creation, that "God desired a dwelling in the lower realms."[6]

In the spiritual service of every individual there must also be a fusion of the "upper realms" and the "lower realms," the body and

---

6. *Sefer Hama'amarim* 5735, "*Vekibeil haYehudim,*" and 5745, "*Kimu vekiblu haYehudim.*" A question arises that if *Purim* is the confirmation of the giving of the Torah, showing that the Jews accepted it willingly, why then do none of the observances seem to reflect this? It can be explained that when a person does something motivated by his own will, he does it with added care and zeal compared to when he is acting under compulsion. This is illustrated in three of the observances of *Purim*, gifts of food to friends, reading the *megillah*, and gifts to the poor, all basic *mitzvot* which have special added aspects on *Purim*. In sending gifts of food to friends, a person performs the mitzvah of *ahavat Yisrael*, loving a fellow Jew, going beyond the minimum requirements of the mitzvah and actively seeking a friend for whom to perform a kindness. Further, he gives his friend food, something he can benefit from immediately, and not money, which would have to be exchanged for something else. In giving charity to the poor during the year, a person is merely forbidden to refrain from giving when he encounters a poor person. On *Purim* the person has to seek out two poor people and give them charity. Similarly, the *megillah* was added to the books of *Tanach* through Esther's special request that it be written down. Moreover, it is read at night, something novel with respect to the usual daytime Torah reading (*Likkutei Sichot*, vol. 16, pp. 365–366).

the soul. *Purim* was also unique in that the Jew demonstrated self-sacrifice with the body. Generally it is the soul, not the body, which has a connection to spirituality. At Sinai the fusion of the spiritual and the physical was divinely initiated, and the elevation experienced by the Jews was mainly spiritual. On *Purim*, by contrast, the Jews sacrificed themselves physically for the sake of God. This resulted in a fusion of the below with the above in which the below was what brought about the connection.

At the giving of the Torah God's voice came from all four directions, and the whole world was silent without even a bird chirping. However, despite the intensity of the revelation, when something comes from "above" there is no change in the "below." This is shown by the verse "when the ram's horn sounds a prolonged tone they shall come up to the mountain,"[7] which indicates that nothing really changed in the mountain after the revelation at Sinai. Immediately after the giving of the Torah, the Jews could ascend the mountain that they were forbidden to ascend immediately beforehand. Just as the mountain did not change, the Jews did not change, as is shown when they made the golden calf not long afterwards. Permanent spiritual revelation, by contrast, only comes through the labor and effort of the ones experiencing the elevation. Also, as we have been saying, God's desire for a "dwelling here below" means this should be through those below refining and elevating themselves to become a vessel for Godliness.

There is another reason that service here below is so crucial. The lowest level has a very high source and can reach a level without limitations. From this we see (as Chasidic philosophy often points out) the advantage of the lowest level.

---

7. Exodus 19:13.

SELF-SACRIFICE

In the self-sacrifice of *Purim* the Jews transcended reason and rationale,[8] for self-sacrifice is not something that makes sense intellectually. Intellect, in fact, presupposes continued existence (i.e., the desire to understand something requires the existence of an "I" doing the understanding). This is also true of the nonintellectual, more emotional character traits. To say "I love something" is also, in a sense, to emphasize the "I."

The Jews, in contrast, stood a whole year in a posture of self-sacrifice higher than rationale. Besides the fact that self-sacrifice is generally not rational, this is especially so when the self-sacrifice is maintained for a whole year. There are many variations in a person's spiritual circumstances in the course of a year, and therefore the Jews demonstrated a super-rational determination to hold the course when they refused to submit to Haman's decree. This super-rational quality is especially relevant, interestingly, to a comparison between *Purim* and the holiday of Yom Kippur.

A DAY LIKE *PURIM*

Yom Kippur (*Yom Hakippurim*) can be read as *Yom kePurim* (a day like *Purim*). Both of them have a similar spiritual service, but the fact that Yom Kippur is being called *Yom kePurim* implies that

---

8. This is why the Jews are always called "*Yehudim*," a name denoting self-sacrifice, throughout the Book of Esther. The Talmud states that "one who denies idolatry is compared to one who affirms, accepts beyond reason ("*modeh*," which is etymologically related to "*Yehudi*") the whole Torah," *Kiddushin* 40a.

Purim is the standard for the comparison and therefore greater than Yom Kippur.[9] On the original Yom Kippur, when the second tablets were given, the Jews were in a lofty spiritual state, while *Purim* took place during the ultimate concealment of holiness, and therefore the Jews' acceptance of the Torah was higher.

There is a further reason that the spiritual service of *Purim* and Yom Kippur are compared: both of them possess the service of a lottery. *Purim* is named after Haman's lottery to find a month in which to carry out his evil decree. Spiritually, a lottery represents service higher than reason and rationale since something chosen by lottery is chosen randomly and not for any reason. Just as on Yom Kippur the service of repentance reaches and involves commitment on the highest levels [see chapter on Yom Kippur], higher than reason and rationale, on *Purim* we commit ourselves to God and the Torah on an essential level, one which transcends reason. This is the explanation for naming the holiday lottery.

---

9. *Torah Or, Megillat Ester*, 92d, 95d, based on *Tikkunei Zohar* 421 (57b). *Torah Or*, it should be noted, states that Yom Kippur is named after *Purim*, implying that *Purim* is higher. *Tikkunei Zohar* states that *Purim* is named after Yom Kippur, implying the opposite, that Yom Kippur is higher, except that when the fasting of Yom Kippur is transformed into celebration in the future, it will resemble *Purim*. (*Sefer Hama'amarim Melukat*, vol. 5, p. 189, note 9).

See also *Sefer Hama'amarim* 5661, p. 219, which notes that Yom Kippur only partially atones for certain sins, which must be further atoned for by suffering. For profaning God's name in public, the atonement process must include Yom Kippur, suffering, and finally death. *Purim*, however, surpasses Yom Kippur in that the Jews profaned God's name publicly when they partook of the feast of Achashverosh, but their sins were completely atoned for without suffering. See also *Sefer Hama'amarim* 5628, p. 110.

AD DELO YADA

The emphasis on self-sacrifice that transcends reason explains one of the famous *Purim* observances. The Talmud[10] states that on *Purim* at the festive meal one is obligated to drink wine "until one cannot tell (*ad delo yada*) the difference between 'cursed be Haman' and 'blessed be Mordechai.'" The holiday of Sukkot is known as the "time of our joy," but nevertheless, in the times when Jewish courts could enforce civil and criminal laws, messengers would be sent to make sure people did not become too drunk. In reference to *Purim*, one might ask, what level of holiness can be reached through drunkenness, and for that matter, isn't this the opposite of holiness? Moreover, what is desirable about not knowing, etc.?

The explanation is that the service of *Purim* every year is to reach the level of transcending reason, the level at which one cannot tell the difference, etc. Haman represents impudent evil, which transcends reason, as indicated by his status as a descendent of the Amalekites, who opposed holiness even knowing they were doomed to failure. The spiritual equivalent of Amalek in every person must be wiped out and this is accomplished through reaching the level of not being able to tell, etc. Then the superrational determination to fulfill God's commandments defeats the irrational stubbornness that motivates disobedience. The essence of the soul is revealed.

In order to understand more deeply the service of not-knowing, of transcending reason, it is necessary to consider the different levels and faculties of the soul. Chasidic philosophy explains that in the make-up of the soul there are ten powers that are called

---

10. *Megillah* 7b.

the inner-powers (*kochot penimim*), intellect and emotions, and higher still are powers that transcend intellect, such as *ratzon* (will) and *ta'anug* (delight). These are called the encompassing powers (*kochot makifim*), and they are also called *lo yada* (that which is not known) in a person since they are usually not revealed. During the year, generally speaking, a Jew performs his spiritual service only with his intellect and emotions, seeking to intellectually understand God's greatness in order to inspire love and fear of God. It can happen, however, that the encompassing powers are still not committed to holiness.

This is exemplified in the Talmud's[11] account of Rabbi Yochanan Ben Zakkai's reaction to his impending demise. He cried, saying "I don't know which way they are taking me," meaning that he did not know if he would be taken to Paradise or Purgatory.

The obvious question is how such a great sage could be in doubt concerning his fate in the afterlife. Chasidic philosophy explains[12] that Rabbi Yochanan Ben Zakkai knew the level of his *kochot penimim*, intellect and emotions, but he did not know the level of his *kochot makifim*, will and delight. Rabbi Yochanan thought it possible that his essential self did not truly love holiness and hate evil because he was too preoccupied with working with his *kochot penimim* to tell. When we drink wine to reach the level of *lo yada* (not knowing) we are seeking to commit the levels of the soul that transcend intellect, and that are connected to the essence of the soul, to holiness. These levels should feel "cursed be Haman" and "blessed be Mordechai"—love of holiness and hatred of evil.

---

11. *Berachot* 28b.
12. See *Or Hatorah, Parshat Pinchas*, entry beginning "*Ach begoral.*"

Attaining the level of not knowing, which a Jew can accomplish on *Purim* for the whole year, is also explained in chasidic philosophy through another approach. The *mitzvah* of drinking to the point of not knowing the difference between cursing Haman and blessing Mordechai is sometimes explained in chasidic literature in a different way. Blessing Mordechai, affirming goodness, corresponds to fulfilling positive commandments. Cursing Haman, rejecting evil, means refraining from the forbidden.

The whole year a person has a different feeling in fulfilling a positive mitzvah than in fulfilling a negative mitzvah. He relates to a positive commandment as something good and to evil as something negative. In observing a positive commandment, he has a feeling of becoming closer to God; abstaining from something prohibited by a negative commandment is an opposite emotion, the fear of rebelling against God and becoming detached from Him.

However, there is a higher way of serving God. When spiritual service transcends reason, the person does not know the difference between these two services, for everything is equal to him. Both negative commandments and positive commandments are viewed as something positive, another opportunity to be close to God.

This is similar to what chasidic philosophy explains concerning why God said the whole Ten Commandments in one expression, even though it is not possible to understand it in this way. It is explained that this is to teach that from God's viewpoint, so to speak, all the Ten Commandments, positive and negative, are one idea. All reveal God's unity and presence in the world, either by increasing holiness or negating what interferes with it. The person obeying the commandments has to carry them out in two ways, but it is only from our standpoint that they are two different categories, positive and negative.

One might still wonder why wine in particular is the means for reaching the level of not knowing. Our Sages say, "When wine enters the secret comes out."[13] Wine's ability to reveal the hidden is symbolized by the fact that wine is initially hidden in the grape and then revealed when the grapes are made into wine.[14] When one has the intention of bringing out one's inner ability to serve God, the Torah gives one the ability to use wine at the festive meal of *Purim* to reach the level in which positive and negative commands are equal. This is the opposite of wanton drunkenness in which wine is used to throw off responsibility, but on the contrary, one uses wine to increase inner commitment to God.

PURIM AND CHANUKAH

On *Purim* it was revealed that nature itself is Godliness, in contrast to *Chanukah*, whose advantage is the great light that illuminates the darkness. The Jews were in the second Temple period when the miracle of *Chanukah* took place, while *Purim* occurred when the Jews were in exile after the destruction of the first Temple. The Syrian Greek war was aimed at destroying the Jewish religion, whereas Haman's decree was directed at the Jews' very existence.[15] The advantage of *Purim* is not the revelation that is elicited, but the advantage of the lowest level itself, as stated above. *Purim* is therefore also specifically associated with *galut*, the period of exile, the time when there is less revelation of di-

---

13. *Eiruvin* 65a; *Sanhedrin* 38a; *Midrash Tanchuma, Shemini* 5; *Zohar* III 39a.

14. *Likkutei Sichot,* vol. 31, p. 179, note 23.

15. While it is true that he gave them a year to repudiate the Jewish religion, his main motivation was his desire to destroy the Jews utterly.

vinity, and thus the greatest revelation of the essence of the Jewish soul when the Jews keep the Torah.

The *Chanukah* miracle and the *Purim* miracle involve two different dimensions of God's greatness. On *Chanukah*, the miracle was that God defied the rules of nature: Although the Jews were weak and few in number, they won the war, which was a supernatural miracle. Since God has no limits, He could break the rules of nature.

The miracle of *Purim* presents the appearance of events simply working out in favor of the Jewish people. This represents the fact that God is capable of fusing opposites: Nature remained nature, and yet a miracle occurred. In a sense, the *Purim* miracle is greater than that of *Chanukah*, for it demonstrates that God can defy the rules of nature and yet enclose a miracle in the garments of nature.

In contrast to *Purim*, the observances of *Chanukah* (see chapter on *Chanukah*) are mainly spiritual, emphasizing the revelation of a brilliant illumination capable of lighting up the darkness of the world. In the more physical celebration of *Purim*, the festive meal, etc., the emphasis is not on God's revelation, but rather on what lies in the hidden or concealed in nature, which ultimately can be even more miraculous than the openly miraculous.

This explains the puzzling fact that *Purim*, named after the Persian word *pur*, is the only holiday with a non-Hebrew name. In the Holy tongue, unlike all other languages, the name of something expresses its spiritual essence. Since only the name of an object in Hebrew expresses its spiritual essence, its name in another language represents the concealment of Godliness. Thus, the use of a Persian name indicates that God did the impossible by making a miracle happen in a hidden way.

Along the same lines, the Talmud states there is a an allusion to Esther in the Torah in a passage referring to a time of exile, when God said, "And I will surely hide (*hasteir astir*) my face."[16] This means the name Esther is related to the word *hester* (concealment) and thus the title of *Megillat Ester* derives from the nature of the miracle.

Moreover, the Book of Esther, among all the other books of the Bible, is unique in not mentioning God's name even once. When we consider that it is customary to begin even a short note or a letter, "by the grace of God," it certainly seems remarkable that an entire book devoted to a miracle should not mention God's name.

The explanation is as follows: When we use God's name, no matter what name we use, it is still a definition and therefore some kind of limitation. For example, the Tetragrammaton represents "He was, He is, and He will be"—in one word—God as He transcends time. Or, as chasidic philosophy explains, this name means *mehaveh* (He creates) and the letter *yud* before the three other letters of God's name means that it is something happening in the present tense. Both interpretations are still definitions: God is beyond time, and He is the Creator, but He cannot ultimately be designated by any name or definition.[17]

A miracle that comes in a hidden way, as stated above, is even greater than an obvious miracle. Since this kind of miracle is beyond nature but in nature, it is an expression of God's essence, which is literally without limitation, not even that of calling Him limitless.

Thus, God's name is not mentioned because the story of Esther represents the essence of God, because only God's essence (beyond designation by any name) can put what is higher than na-

---

16. Deuteronomy 31:18.

17. As the *Zohar* states, God cannot be hinted in a letter, or a crown above a letter.

ture into nature.[18] What brought out this revelation of God's essence on the original *Purim* is that the Jews served God from their own essence. That is why the spiritual service of every *Purim* is to reveal our essence through "not knowing the difference," etc.

The fact that God's essence is revealed through the spiritual service and effort of the lowest levels explains the statement of our Sages[19] that all the holidays will be nullified when *Mashiach* comes except *Purim*. Similarly it is written concerning the Book of Esther that all the *Megillot* (Esther, Ruth, Lamentations, Ecclesiastes, and the Song of Songs) will be nullified except for Esther.[20] Given that it is not possible to speak of the nullification of holidays when no *mitzvot* will ever be changed or nullified, Chasidic philosophy explains that "nullified" here means something different. The future nullification of the holidays is analogous to what happens to the light of a candle in the daylight: Since the sunlight is so bright during the day, the light of the candle is not noticed. Thus, due to the great light that will shine when *Mashiach* comes the light of the holidays will not be felt so much, except for *Purim*, which represents a light even greater than that of the giving of the Torah. *Purim* fulfills the intention of the giving of the Torah, that God desired that His essence should be revealed here below.

---

18. This points to another dimension of "not knowing the difference between 'cursed be Haman,' and 'blessed be Mordechai,'" which means appreciation of Godliness beyond names, and thus beyond definitions.

19. *Midrash* Proverbs 9:2; *Yalkut Shemoni, remez* 944.

20. *Sefer Hama'amarim* 5735, *Vekibeil haYehudim*, and 5745, *Kimu vekiblu haYehudim*.

8

⁊

Pesach: The Birthday of the Jewish People

". . . and on that very day all the hosts of God went out of the land of Egypt." (Exodus 12:41)

Pesach is the first of the three pilgrim festivals mentioned in the Bible (the other two are *Shavuot* and Sukkot), and it is called the "Head of all the pilgrim festivals." Just as with Rosh Hashanah (which means "Head of the Year"), head means more than first. The general life-force of the body is in the brain, which controls the whole body. Thus, just as Rosh Hashanah is the general life-force of the whole year, *Pesach* is the general life-force of the three pilgrim festivals. In addition, *Pesach* is considered the birthday of the Jewish nation; for that reason, too, the other two festivals are considered the maturation and development that follows the "birth" on *Pesach*.

YETZIAT MITZRAIM—THE EXODUS FROM EGYPT

Pesach commemorates the amazing liberation of the Jewish people from Egypt, which the *Midrash* identifies as a place from which no slave ever managed to escape.[1]

Chasidic philosophy, however, explains that the Hebrew word for Egypt, *Mitzrayim*, is etymologically related to the word *meitzarim* (limitations or boundaries). In the liberation from *Mitzrayim*, the Jews were not only physically freed from bondage, but God also gave the Jewish nation the ability to achieve a spiritual liberation. The spiritual exodus from Egypt is the quintessential theme of the holiday, as we shall see.

The concept of the spiritual Exodus from Egypt involves the two souls of a Jew, one of the basic concepts of chasidic philosophy. A Jew possesses a Godly soul, which is united with God and only concerned with spirituality, and an animal soul, which is only concerned with gratifying physical drives. The Godly soul is said to be in prison by being clothed in the body, which is subject to the influence of the animal soul. The exodus of the Godly soul from its prison (from *Mitzraim* as an expression of *meitzarim*) occurs when the person engages in learning Torah and fulfilling *mitzvot*, for then the Godly soul is in control of the body and no longer dominated by the animal soul. The ultimate liberation of the Godly soul will occur when *Mashiach* comes and evil is completely destroyed.

The exodus of the Godly soul from its prison in the body is explained in *Tanya*[2] in connection with the verse "the people fled." At first glance this is surprising: Why did they have to flee? Wasn't

---

1. *Mechilta*, Exodus 18:11.
2. Chapter 31.

Pharoah totally defeated and compelled to let them simply leave? Actually this refers to the spiritual state of the Jewish people at the time. The Jewish people were strongly affected by the corruption of Egypt and corresponding to their physical state of exile, their Godly souls were also in a state of subjugation. This was a condition that did not end until the giving of the Torah, but even in Egypt they still had a desire and yearning to escape from this spiritual state and achieve closeness to God. Since they were still in the throes of evil, they had to flee, to simply remove themselves from the evil without trying to contend with it.

The *Tanya*[3] also explains the concept of the spiritual Exodus from Egypt as it relates to an individual's daily spiritual service of God. Our Sages state that "in every generation a person is obligated to regard himself as if he had just left Egypt."[4] Rabbi Schneur Zalman goes farther and states that this applies not only to every generation but to *every day*. Through keeping *mitzvot*, and specifically through reciting the *Shema*, which expresses the soul's complete dedication and subservience to God, the Godly soul experiences an exodus from its prison in the animal soul.

Chasidic philosophy also explains[5] the language of the verse, "As in the days of the exodus from Egypt I will show you wonders."[6] We might ask, why does it say days when the Exodus was in one day? Chasidic philosophy explains that during the period between Exodus from Egypt and the future redemption a Jew must depart from new limitations every day. The achievements of yesterday are limitations relative to what must be accomplished

---

3. Chapter 47.
4. *Pesachim* 116b.
5. *Sefer Hama'amarim* 5740, "*Kimei tzeitcha.*"
6. Micah 7:15.

today so that there is a constant obligation to transcend previous accomplishments. Thus, as long as a person is still limited in some way, he is in *Mitzraim* (*meitzarim*). This is why the verse refers to days in the plural: The concept of the Exodus continues every day.

THE FOOD OF FAITH

The theme of the liberation of the Godly soul from the animal soul is particularly emphasized in the eating of *matzah* and avoidance of *chametz* on *Pesach*. In order to understand this, it is necessary to investigate the general topic of *chametz* and *matzah*.

The commandment of not eating *chametz* on *Pesach* is unique in that the day before *Pesach*, and the day after the close of the festival, it is permissible to eat *chametz*, whereas on *Pesach* it is forbidden, so much so that we are not only prohibited from eating *chametz*, but even from owning it. This is underscored by the fact that on *Shavuot,* fifty days later, it is not only permissible to eat *chametz*, but the main sacrifice of the day is the offering of two loaves of bread in the Temple. The contrast of a forbidden status on one holiday and a mandatory status on the next is especially interesting considering that *Shavuot* is the culmination of *Pesach*.

In the same way, the biblical commandment to eat *matzah* on *Pesach* night requires investigation. The *Haggadah* states that the Jews rushed out of Egypt and had no chance to let their dough rise. The Torah, however, relates that the Jews were commanded to eat *matzah before* midnight on the night of their departure, and *before* they rushed out of Egypt.

Although according to many commentaries, God commanded the Jews to eat *matzah* before midnight, knowing that they would be rushed out of Egypt after midnight, obviously, there must be some further significance for eating *matzah* other than the Jews' leaving Egypt in a hurry.

In addition, why, of all the details of the Exodus, is the Jews' haste to leave so worthy of commemoration that it becomes *mandatory* to eat *matzah*? What is the significance of their haste?

The *Zohar*[7] states that *matzah* is "the food of faith," which means that eating *matzah* actually causes one's faith to be strengthened. The *Sefer Hachinnuch* writes that the commandment to relate the exodus of Egypt is a

> full indication and proof of the creation of the world out of nonexistence, and that there is a pre-existent God with the will and power who gives all created things their being . . . and He is able to change them as He may wish at any particular time, just as He did in Egypt when He altered the world's ways of nature for our sake.[8]

Even though this is written to simply indicate that by performing the commandments of *Pesach* we create a commemoration of the events of the Exodus of Egypt, establishing faith in God in our hearts, the Torah has both a mystical and a revealed dimension. The *Sefer Hachinnuch* is concerned with the revealed dimension of Torah, but according to mysticism *matzah* itself has the power to strengthen faith.

To understand this, we must first explore the concept of faith. It is not necessary to have faith that God gives existence to the world even though we cannot actually see the process by which He does this. Similarly, a person does not have to have faith that he is alive since he can observe that his body has life, and obvi-

---

7. *Zohar Vayeitze* 157.

8. *Mitzvah* no.21 (*Parshat Bo*).

ously otherwise it would be inanimate. He can, in fact, be just as certain of the existence of the spiritual life-force that is invested in his body as he would be if he could see it, even though his soul has no physical form. Along these lines it is written, "From my flesh I see God."[9] Thus, just as one sees the life of the soul by seeing the life of the body, similarly one "sees" the life that enlivens and gives existence to the world, which is a large body. Each entity in the world is inanimate in itself, but each one has a life-force so that, for instance, the Earth has the power to make plants grow, the heavenly bodies are able to move, etc. This is so because God "fills the whole world" and confers the various powers possessed by each created entity. No faith is necessary at all for this, and the righteous of the nations and their wise men also understand it.

However, the faith that is unique to the Jewish people is expressed in the first commandment "I am the Lord, your God," which refers to the full extent of God's existence, that He is exalted and transcendent and far beyond the level of being a life-giver. When a person achieves the realization that God is infinitely beyond giving existence to the world, then the world is revealed to have no significance. Chasidic philosophy compares the Godly life-force that gives life to the world to a mere ray of light that has little significance compared to the sun, God Himself. The ray of light is totally dependent on the sun and is actually no more than a revelation of the sun's existence. Nevertheless, a ray of light that has radiated beyond the sun does have a discernible existence apart from the sun.

A more apt comparison for a created entity is a ray of light that has not yet radiated and that is still within the globe of the sun,

---

9. Job 19:26.

since God is the only true existence and there is actually nothing outside of Him. A created entity is thus completely absorbed within its source, like a ray of the sun within the sun, and it has no true independent existence. The faith that is implied in the commandment "I am the Lord your God" is, thus, faith in God's essence, which is not clothed in the world as the soul is in the body. One should believe that the world and everything it contains are totally dependent on God and essentially nothing without Him, unlike the body, which has a certain significance apart from the soul.[10]

And this is the mitzvah of eating *matzah* that the Jews were commanded in Egypt, because in Egypt they lacked this faith in God's absolute transcendence. At the Exodus their state is compared in the Torah to that of a newborn child.[11] To bring the Jewish people from this state to the true faith, which is associated with adulthood, *matzah* was necessary, which is called *michlah deheimnuta* (food of faith).

This association of *matzah* and faith accords with the saying of our Sages "A child does not know how to call 'father' and 'mother' until it tastes grain."[12] The child's calling is not true knowledge of his father's identity, which involves knowing that his father engendered him and that the father naturally loves his son and feeds him and provides all his needs—the child does not know all this; he only calls father and the true concept is higher than his knowledge and understanding. Nevertheless, we do not say that he has not achieved any recognition of who his father is, for he obviously recognizes him, and he will not demonstrate filial affection to anyone else.

---

10. See *Derech Mitzvotecha, Hashbatat Chametz Ve'achilat Matzah*.

11. Ezekiel 16:6–7.

12. *Berachot* 40a.

This means that this true knowledge that is higher than his childish understanding is actually present in the child's knowledge in a reduced form. We can even say that through this he actually intuitively grasps the true concept of fatherhood, except that it has been brought down to his level. The process by which the true concept of fatherhood is condensed into the child's ability to call father is initiated by the taste of grain.[13]

The concept of the faith conferred by *matzah*, which must be made from grain, is similar. Through eating *matzah* the true knowledge of God is drawn into the souls of the Jewish people according to their capacity to grasp it. Thus, they call to their Father in heaven; that is, they achieve faith in God's essence, which is far more exalted than what can be surmised from mere observation that He gives life to the world. They realize that truly the whole world is literally nothing in the face of God's existence; the world is not even an existence that is secondary to God's.

In truth, every Jew believes this with a true faith, one that will never budge, to the point that he is able to give his life to sanctify God's name.[14] Nevertheless, he does not fully understand God's nature, so that his knowledge is analogous to a child calling father. Ultimately what the child means when he calls father does actually embody the essence of the adult concept of fatherhood, as we have been saying. Nevertheless, since it is not possible to intellectually understand the whole truth, this is essentially a matter of faith.

---

13. The explanation for this is that the source of wheat is the divine attribute of *da'at*—knowledge (*chita*—wheat—has the numerical value of twenty-two, corresponding to the number of letters in the Hebrew alphabet). We also find an opinion in the Talmud that the fruit of the tree of knowledge was wheat.

14. True self-sacrifice is not based on intellect, but rather based on faith that God far transcends simply being the Creator.

This is demonstrated by *matzah*, which is simply flour and water, and which does not rise. Rising represents ego, or at least involving one's *own* intellect and emotion in one's spiritual service. The person's own intellect and emotion are properties of the animalistic soul, associated with *yeshut*, the sense of the self as an independent entity. One might suppose that the intellect, at least, is objective and unconnected to ego; however, when a person understands something intellectually, there is still an involvement of the self. His understanding is precisely that: *his* understanding. However, *matzah*, which doesn't rise and has no other ingredients, besides flour and water, represents simplistic, pure dedication and *bitul* (self nullification)—the opposite of *yeshut*. *Matzah*, lacking leaven, does not have the taste of bread, and the word for taste in Hebrew, *ta'am*, also means reason. Therefore, *matzah*, without the *ta'am* of bread, symbolizes commitment beyond reason. Bread, in contrast, is associated with *chachmah* (wisdom)—a level of understanding that can only be conveyed to a fully grown adult, who has the capacity for it.

This is also why on *Pesach*, the birth of the Jewish nation, there can be no association with leavened bread, for the foundation of the Jewish people's existence is a pure commitment deeper than logic, as they demonstrated when they received the Torah, saying, "*Na'aseh venishmah*"—"We will do [all of the commandments of the Torah] and [then] we will understand."

So, too, on the holiday of *Pesach*, there is no room for rationale or ego, and without the proper foundation there can be no further development.[15]

---

15. Nevertheless, a proper foundation alone is insufficient. We are expected to also involve our intellect and emotions so that they, too, should be stimulated in the service to God, thus enabling a recognition of the beauty of Judaism.

Just as we were commanded in the actual eating of *matzah* in the exodus from Egypt, so are we commanded to eat *matzah* in all generations, in order to make the above-discussed faith in God's absolute transcendence permanent. It is necessary for the person to experience the spiritual exodus from Egypt every day, but in the year as a whole, a special ability is granted on *Pesach* to the Godly soul, enabling it to refine the animal soul and to permanently imbue it with the special faith of a Jewish person, as discussed above. This is all through the eating of *matzah*.

CHAMETZ AND MATZAH

As stated above, on *Pesach* we not only eat *matzah*, but we avoid *chametz*. Besides the fact that *chametz* rises and *matzah* does not, the difference is expressed in a second way:

The words *chametz* and *matzah* are spelled with the same letters except that *matzah* is spelled with a *hei*, while *chametz* contains a *chet*. The letter *hei* is similar to the letter *chet* since they are both formed from three lines and open at the bottom. The difference is only in the *chet* being closed on three sides completely while the *hei* has an opening above.

The closedness of the *chet* can be associated with the saying "sin crouches at the door,"[16] and the form of the letter implies that there is no escape from sin, since the opening is closed. The opening in the top of the *hei* implies that although the situation is that "sin crouches at the door," still there is an opening above and it is possible to escape a sinful state and repent.

---

16. Genesis 4:7.

The distinction between humility and arrogance and closedness and openness are actually interrelated, for when a person feels humble, even if he sinned he will be open to thoughts of repentance, but when he is arrogant and conceited he is unlikely to change his ways. When he is humble he does not strive to justify his reprehensible behavior and he judges himself fairly. And when he realizes that his behavior is not as it should be, he repents. In contrast, as a consequence of being closed up, the person finds ways of justifying all his actions.

In a similar vein, the chasidic master Rabbi Menachem Nachum of Chernoble writes in connection to the prohibition of eating *mashehu* (the slightest amount) of *chametz* that *kedushah* (holiness) is called *matzah* and that *kelipah* (evil) is called *chametz*. There is only a *mashehu* between the letters *hei* and *chet*, and sometimes the two letters are even interchanged. The *yeitzer hara* (evil inclination) does not make a direct attempt to cause a person to sin, but rather he tries to disguise a sin as a mitzvah. He tries, in other words, to change the *hei* into a *chet*. Thus, a person must be careful about even a *mashehu* of *chametz*, he must resist the subtle machinations of the *yeitzer hara*.[17]

The concept that *chametz* represents ego because it rises can help us more deeply understand the statement in the *Haggadah* that associates eating *matzah* with being rushed out of Egypt. Even though the dough did not, in fact, have time to rise, this detail alone is not what we are commemorating. During the Exodus there was a great midnight revelation that God is the only existence, which left no possibility for the feeling of ego or individual autonomy. This even manifested itself physically so that the dough was affected.

---

17. *Ma'or Einaim, Parshat Tzav.*

In the Exodus, the Jews ate two different kinds of *matzah*—the *matzah* before midnight that gave the Jews the recognition of God as our Father; and the *matzah* after midnight, resulting from the revelation of God's unity. However, once we received the Torah on Mount Sinai, the mitzvah of eating *matzah* became much greater than that before Sinai in Egypt. Now, on the holiday, even before midnight, we experience the same holiness as the revelation of midnight during the exodus. That is why, until this day, we say, "the *matzah* we eat is because of the *matzah* the Jews ate when they were rushed out of Egypt."

We can now understand why *chametz* is forbidden on *Pesach*, but permitted later on (and even mandatory on *Shavuot*). On *Pesach*, the emphasis is on the liberation of the Godly soul from the animal soul, which is in its full strength and still unrefined. However, after the counting of the *Omer*, the animal soul is refined to the point that it, too, desires holiness, and ultimately a person is supposed to employ all his faculties in the service of God. This process of refinement takes place during *Sefirat Ha'omer*.

A person has seven emotional faculties, the primary components of the whole range of human expression and experience. These correspond to the seven *sefirot*, the divine faculties through which God created the world. Each one of the seven emotions is in turn compounded of all seven, so that there are forty-nine in all: kindness of kindness, severity of kindness, mercy of kindness, etc. During each day between *Pesach* and *Shavuot* a Jew is able to examine and refine one attribute. As he gradually climbs the ladder of self-refinement he becomes more in tune with the divine attributes and after the forty-nine days is completed he has come as close as humanly possible to becoming worthy of receiving the Torah.

This also, incidentally, explains some of the puzzling aspects of *Sefirat Ha'omer*. In the days of the Temple, the actual offering of the *Omer* consisted of barley, which is usually thought of as food for animals. As a matter of fact, the offering brought by a *sotah*, a woman suspected of adultery, is barley, in order to emphasize that her actions were those of an animal. However, the use of barley for the *Omer* offering emphasizes that *Sefirat Ha'omer* is a process of refining the *animal* soul. This is also emphasized in the word used for counting (*sefirah*). According to the Maggid of Mezeritch, the word *sefirah* is related to the word *sapirut* (brilliance or illumination).[18] A person is supposed to refine the attributes of his animal soul until it is possible for the Godly light to shine within them.

THE NAME *PESACH*

The process of gradually refining the animal soul takes place, for the most part, after the conclusion of the holiday. The word *Pesach*, however, refers to the initial stage of the Jews' liberation from Egypt, and it is necessary to understand how this relates to the spiritual liberation from Egypt that we have been discussing. The *Hagaddah* states that the word *Pesach* is a reference to the biblical account of the events leading up to the Exodus, which states that God passed over the Jewish homes and struck the first-born male Egyptians.

This suggests several questions. The Ba'al Shem Tov teaches that every letter in the Hebrew alphabet embodies a certain Godly force, and a word is a combination of forces that make up the essence of the created entity named by the word. Thus, a holiday's Hebrew name expresses its essence. In the case of *Pesach*, the

---

18. *Likkutei Torah, Emor,* 35b.

passing over and sparing of the homes of the firstborn Jewish males is only one detail of the general miracle of the Jews' liberation from Egypt. Why, then, is the essence of the whole holiday indicated by the name *Pesach*?

Furthermore, the idea of passing over itself needs explanation. God controls everything in the world, including the most minute detail. If God wants to have a particular effect on a particular group of houses, then they are already immediately subject to his influence. What does it mean to say that he passes over something? We are also told that the Jews made a sign on their doorposts, as if God somehow needed a sign to distinguish between the Jews and the Egyptians.

Throughout chasidic philosophy the concept is stressed that every event in the physical world happens first in the spiritual world. On *Pesach*, then, there was a passing over in some sense on the spiritual level that lead to a passover on a physical level. This can be explained as follows: God created the world so that man would benefit from God's kindness and life-force based on his own efforts. As man refines himself, he becomes a vessel for successively higher levels of revelation.[19] On every level, in fact, the more refined the world is, the more light (i.e., Godliness) it can appreciate.

The stages through which man passes as he refines himself are known as the fifty gates of holiness (wisdom), and each one is associated with one of the forty-nine days between *Pesach* and *Shavuot*, which are the forty-nine days of *Sefirat Ha'omer*, and the fiftieth day, the holiday of *Shavuot* itself. During this period, as

---

19. Adam and Eve's fate illustrates what happens when man is undeserving. When they ate the forbidden fruit, they were no longer fit for the great spiritual energy of the Garden of Eden.

we have seen, a Jew's task is to refine himself to the point to which he is worthy to receive the Torah on *Shavuot*. (The spiritual service of *Sefirat Ha'omer* is a process of refinement in which the animalistic soul is convinced that Godliness is good for it, so that ultimately on *Shavuot* the Godly soul and the animalistic soul become unified in their desires.)

However, just as there are fifty gates of holiness, there are fifty gates of impurity, in which the fiftieth gate is the lowest level. As the Jewish people dwelled in Egypt for 210 years, they gradually descended to the forty-ninth level of impurity, and if they had stayed in Egypt a moment longer, it would have been impossible to extract them—the liberation of the Godly soul from the animal soul would no longer have been possible. Therefore, God had to pass over His own divine system rather than let the Jews earn the necessary great revelation. God, in His infinite mercy (*Targum Onkelos* translates the word *Pesach*, [God] passed over, as had mercy),[20] passed over His own system of successive refinement. God Himself, "not an angel or a messenger,"[21] took the Jews out of Egypt, which was the lowest point of impurity, so that we would eventually be lifted up to His level at the giving of the Torah. The Alter Rebbe, Rabbi Schneur Zalman of Liadi, employs the following analogy to describe this whole sequence:

> . . . a great and mighty king shows his great and intense love for a commoner who is despised and lowly among men, a disgraceful creature cast on the dunghill, yet he [the king] comes down to him from the place of his glory, together with all his retinue, and raises him and exalts him from his dunghill and

---

20. Exodus 12:27.

21. The significance of this is that the Jewish people had sunk to such a low point that only God could get them out.

brings him into his palace, the royal palace, into the innermost chamber, such a place that no servant or minister ever enters, and there shares the closest companionship with him with embraces and kisses and spiritual attachment with all his heart and soul.[22]

This is the true essence of *Pesach* that sets the tone of the whole year. When we are on a low spiritual level, we can invoke God's mercy once again, as when He took us out of Egypt. Therefore, the spiritual *Pesach* originally manifested itself as a physical passing over. Since the Jews (under influence of the Egyptians) were on such a low spiritual level, one can argue that they were not worthy of the spiritual liberation of *Pesach*, yet God, in His infinite mercy, spared them. Since they nevertheless had to demonstrate somehow that their essence remained loyal to God, they were commanded to perform the *mitzvot* of circumcision and to prepare the paschal lamb. Since circumcision involves a certain obvious self-sacrifice and since killing sheep, the idol of Egypt, was an affront to Egyptian society, the Jews thus demonstrated the requisite loyalty. We can now answer our earlier question as to the purpose of the sign of blood on the houses. When the Jews put the blood on their doorposts and lintels, their sacrifice gained significance by being embodied in a sign; it was not that God needed a sign, obviously, to tell one home from another.

Another reason for the name *Pesach* is as follows: The holiday of Sukkot comes after the preparation of return to God on Rosh Hashanah and Yom Kippur, and similarly *Shavuot* follows the preparation of *Sefirat Ha'omer*, as we have explained. Similarly, the type of *Shabbat* a person experiences is based on his preparation throughout the six weekdays. The holiday of *Pesach*, however,

---

22. *Tanya*, ch. 46.

comes with no preparation at all. Just as in the Exodus, God took the initiative and jumped over his own system of refinement.

In a deeper sense, *Pesach* is also so named because God reveals His essence on a level that is beyond preparation, thus passing over any orderly progression from higher levels to lower ones. Revelation from the highest level does not come as a result of our work because everything is utterly equal compared to infinity: The number 1000 is not any closer to infinity than one. Thus, every level is equally distant from God's essence. In that sense, *Pesach* is unique in expressing a light that is so great that no preparation or refinements are of any consequence.

SHEVI'I SHEL PESACH

Shevi'i Shel Pesach—the seventh day of *Pesach*, a biblical holiday, is the anniversary of the splitting of the Red Sea, the culmination of the Exodus from Egypt. According to the revealed dimension of the Torah, the splitting of the sea was the completion of the Exodus from Egypt because once the Egyptian army drowned, there was no longer any question of the Egyptians returning the Jewish people to captivity in Egypt. According to chasidic philosophy, however, the splitting of the sea in itself was a highly significant occurrence, even without the events that took place as the Egyptians pursued the Jewish people through the divided waters and then drowned. As is frequently explained in chasidic philosophy, just as the splitting of the sea was a preparation for the original giving of the Torah, every year, the holiday of *Shevi'i Shel Pesach* is a preparation for the spiritual giving of the Torah every *Shavuot*. In order to understand this, we must investigate the miracle itself of the splitting of the sea.

THE SPLITTING OF THE SEA

The splitting of the Red Sea is the quintessential example of God's ability to suspend the laws of nature. The Talmud uses the expression "as difficult as the splitting of the Red Sea" to refer to other divine acts that express God's transcendence and omnipotence.

The classic commentators ask a number of questions about the talmudic and midrashic explanation of this miraculous event. The most basic question concerns the purpose of splitting the Sea in the first place, especially since passing through the Red Sea did not take the Jews closer to their destination in Israel. The Talmud tells us that the Jews went down the shore of the sea and came up on the same side, as if making a huge U turn.[23] Moreover, God obviously did not have to split the Red Sea to drown the Egyptians; He could have simply stopped creating them, instantly canceling their existence.

Another detail in the *Midrash* is puzzling: The waters of the Red Sea and *all* the waters of *all* the seas, even water in drinking glasses, turned into a solid substance. Given that God does not perform miracles without reason, chasidic philosophy asks, what purpose was served by solidifying all the waters in all of the seas? We also find that when the Jews were passing through the Red Sea they experienced revelation and became prophets, to the extent that "even a maidservant saw a greater vision than Ezekiel the prophet."[24] Why should such a thing have occurred then, of all times, when the Jews were struggling to maintain their very existence?

---

23. *Arachin* 15a, *Tosafot*, entry beginning *Kesheim*.
24. *Mechilta*, Exodus 15:2.

Chasidic philosophy asks a question based on the famous statement in the *Pesach Haggadah*, "If He had split the sea and not caused us to cross on the dry land it would have been enough for us." Since the implication is that God's splitting of the Red Sea is itself a benevolent act, what was the benevolence?[25]

Chasidic philosophy views the parting of the Red Sea as the major preparation for the revelation of Sinai, which took place six weeks later. Each created thing, its nature and its form, has its source in the spiritual realm in a much higher state, and through the progressive chain-like descent of spiritual levels, it finally assumes a physical form as well. If an apple is red, sweet, and round, then spiritually speaking it originated from a source possessing the spiritual equivalent of redness, sweetness, and roundness. The apple in the physical world is thus only a manifestation, in all its details, of what the apple means in the spiritual realm.

Similarly every created entity's true existence begins on the spiritual plane and materializes ultimately in physical form. The concept of sea and land, therefore, does not begin in this physical world, but rather from the spiritual existence of sea and land.

On the physical level, as our Sages state, "everything found on the earth can also be found under the water,"[26] and this is also true in the spiritual realm. There are, however, some important distinctions. The creatures under the water, for instance, are swallowed up in the water and covered by it, and therefore they are concealed from the human eye, while everything on the land is readily obvious. The creatures under the water receive their life

---

25. *Ma'amarei Admor Ha'emtza'i, Derushim LePesach*, p. 368.

26. *Chulin* 127a, *Yerushalmi Shabbat* 14:1. Corresponding to the horse is the sea horse and so forth.

directly from the water and therefore perish immediately when removed from it, whereas land-dwelling creatures receive their life only indirectly from the earth and do not have to maintain direct contact with it.[27]

In order to understand the spiritual significance of these two distinctions we must first consider the basic circumstances of creation. The Ba'al Shem Tov explains[28] the verse, "Forever, O God, Your word stands firm in the heavens"[29] to mean that the actual divine words of the ten utterances through which the world was created (such as "Let there be light") continue to exist.[30] Rabbi Schneur Zalman of Liadi expounds on the words of the Ba'al Shem Tov, adding not just that everything is dependent on God, but that everything has its own particular life-force. He continues, "If the letters were to depart even for an instant, God forbid, and return to their source, all the heavens would become naught and absolute nothingness, and it would be as though they had never existed at all."[31] The major implication of this perspective is that God is the only existence. Rabbi Schneur Zalman, by way of analogy, compares the created-Creator relationship to the relationship of rays of sunlight to the sun itself. The light is merely a revelation of the sun itself and ultimately has no independent identity apart from the sun. When the rays of the sun are within the globe of the sun, they do not even have the appearance of a separate iden-

---

27. *Ma'amarei Admor Ha'emtza'i, Derushim LePesach*, p. 370.

28. Cited in *Tanya, Sha'ar Hayichud Veha'emunah*, beg. ch. 1.

29. Psalms 119:89.

30. Although this is stated in *Midrash Tehillim* (*loc. cit.*), the Ba'al Shem Tov expounded upon it and especially emphasized it and disseminated it.

31. *Sha'ar Hayichud Vehaemunah*, ch. 1.

tity, and they only acquire the identity of rays when the radiate into the space that the sun does not occupy.[32]

The spiritual sea represents a level on which the divine creative force that maintains the existence of the worlds is revealed, an energy that normally must be concealed from us since that is the only way in which we can perceive ourselves as independently existing beings. The angels who live in the world that corresponds to the sea are (like the rays of the sun within the globe of the sun) so aware of their Creator that they are completely absorbed within His existence and thus could never depart from that level. In contrast, land, spiritually speaking, indicates a level on which the Godliness that gives life to created entities is removed and concealed. Human beings appear and feel themselves to be separate beings that are not dependent on anything else (analogous to rays of sunlight that have radiated beyond the sun), just as the creatures of the land are not swallowed up and covered by the land, and they are thus not constantly aware of their Creator.

Since, at the revelation of Sinai, the Jews were going to experience a revelation of God's essence, the most monumental relation that could ever occur, it was first necessary to spiritually prepare them by giving them a greater revelation than any one they had hitherto experienced, one which would serve as a foretaste of the even greater revelation that would follow at Sinai. God essentially opened up the spiritual sea that was always concealed from man, allowing the spiritual realm to become openly revealed, just as the creations on land are obvious to us. Since the physical water and land have their true essence in the spiritual land and sea, when God opened the spiritual sea, automatically all waters

---

32. *Sha'ar Hayichud Vehaemunah*, ch. 3.

were affected, including the sea through which the Jewish people passed. This is why the Jewish people were then comparable to Prophets, not as an additional occurrence, but as part of the essential event of the sea splitting.

The Jewish people witnessed the word of God giving life to all of creation, which is normally only revealed to the creatures of the water, the angels. However, unlike the angels, who do not sense themselves as having an existence independent of God, the Jewish people retained a sense of independent existence. This is the explanation of why the *Haggadah* states that if God had merely split the sea without taking the Jews across on dry land, "it would have been enough" (i.e., a kindness). God allowed the Jewish people to see what is normally hidden without becoming totally nullified and losing their identity.

Now one can understand the divine purpose for splitting the sea—not to allow the Jews to come closer to Israel, and not in order to get rid of the Egyptians, but rather to fulfill a special purpose, the opening of the spiritual sea. This is why water changed its form, because the spiritual source of water also changed its form.

We are also now in a position to appreciate another dimension of *Shevi'i Shel Pesach*, which is called "the New Year of self-sacrifice" according to chasidic philosophy. At the moment when the Red Sea split and God told the Jewish people to keep going, Nachshon, who was the elder of the tribe of Yehudah, jumped into the water, and the splitting of the Red Sea occurred.

Chasidic philosophy explains that self-sacrifice and the splitting of the sea are expressions of the same spiritual concept. Just as the splitting of the Red Sea revealed the normally-hidden spiritual world, self-sacrifice reveals what is hidden in the soul. One a Jew reveals the levels of the soul that are unified with God and totally subservient to Him, he then has no concern for his selfish interests and is willing to do whatever is necessary to serve God. On every *Shevi'i shel Pesach* the splitting of the spiritual sea occurs anew. This means that the worlds that were unknown and hidden throughout the year are revealed on that day. What is required of us to benefit from the revelation of the hidden spiritual worlds is the commitment of self-sacrifice.

ACHARON SHEL PESACH—THE LAST DAY OF PESACH

Simply speaking, *Acharon Shel Pesach* is the second day of *Shevi'i Shel Pesach* outside of the land of Israel. Thus, as a continuation of *Shevi'i Shel Pesach*, it is also connected to the splitting of the Red Sea, although it brings out a new dimension of the miracle. Besides being a preparation for the giving of the Torah, this miracle is also associated with redemption, and this is in two respects:

1. It is the completion and perfection of the Exodus from Egypt, for then "And Israel saw the Egyptians dead on the seashore."[33] As it says in the *Tosefta*:[34] "The Exodus and the splitting of the sea should be recalled [in *Emet veyatziv*, the first blessing after the evening *Shema*], since the completion of the redemption was at the splitting of the sea."[35] This is the reason that *Shevi'i Shel Pesach* is not a holiday in its own right, since its central theme is the completion and perfection of the Exodus.

---

33. Exodus 14:30.
34. *Berachot*, ch. 2.
35. *Chasdei David* on the *Tosefta* loc. cit.

2. The miracle resembled the future redemption when, "I will remove the spirit of impurity from the earth."[36] The complete destruction of evil is also associated with the destruction of the Egyptians, for "not one of them remained."[37] This is one of the reasons that prophecies concerning the Third Temple are included in the "Song at the Sea." For instance, we learn that God Himself will build the Third Temple, "The sanctuary which Your hands established." The song also refers to the time when "God will rule for ever and ever,"[38] and immediately at the beginning of the song "*Az yashir Moshe*" there is a hint to the concept of the resurrection of the dead.[39]

Chasidic philosophy explains that this second aspect especially relates to *Acharon Shel Pesach*. As distinguished from *Shevi'i Shel Pesach*, the completion and perfection of the Exodus from Egypt, *Acharon Shel Pesach* is the holiday of the last redemption.[40] Chasidic philosophy explains that the first two days of *Pesach* are the celebration of the fact that God took the Jewish people out of Egypt. The last days of *Pesach* in general, and *Acharon Shel Pesach* in particular, are connected to celebration of the future redemption through *Mashiach*. This is why we find that the last days of

---

36. Zecharia 13:2.

37. Exodus 14:28.

38. Exodus 15:17, 18.

39. *Sanhedrin* 91b. "*Az yashir*" means literally that Moses "will sing," not that "he sang," as would be appropriate in reference to the exodus from Egypt. The Talmud therefore concludes that this is an allusion to the future redemption, which will be followed by the resurrection of the dead, so that Moses "will sing."

40. See also *Sefer Hasichot* 5700, p. 72.

Pesach are celebrated more joyously than the first days. We might wonder why we do not recite the blessing *Shehechiyanu*, which is associated with joyous occasions, on these days. Since *Shevi'i Shel Pesach* is a continuation and completion of the Exodus from Egypt, we do not say the blessing, for we already said it at the beginning of the holiday. The concept of *Acharon Shel Pesach* is that there *will be* a *ge'ulah*, and even though the future redemption will be greater without comparison to the original Exodus to the point that it is in a completely new category, it is not possible to say *Shehechiyanu* on the future *ge'ulah* (redemption). This blessing is only said on rejoicing from something that exists in actuality now, when we are still in a time prior to the redemption—and on the contrary the mention of the redemption causes great pain, for all the appointed times have already passed and *Mashiach* still has not come.[41]

Acharon Shel Pesach is the eighth day of the festival of *Pesach*. Chasidic philosophy explains the significance of the number eight in reference to *Chanukah* when we light an eight-branched menorah. The world was created through the seven divine emotional attributes, one of which shone on each of the original days of creation, and the number eight stands for a level beyond the limits of the world.[42] Although eight is beyond seven, since it is the eighth with respect to the seven, it retains a connection with the number seven and influences it. Hence, the number eight represents drawing the infinite—eight—into the finite—seven—bringing Godliness to the limited mundane world.

Acharon Shel Pesach is also unique in being designated *acharon* (the last). This quality is also expressed in connection to the tribe

---

41. *Likkutei Sichot*, vol. 37, "*Yamim Acharonin shel Pesach.*"
42. *Teshuvat Rashba*, vol. 1, sec. 9.

of Dan. The tribe of Dan was the last in the formation of the tribes when traveling in the desert and its members collected all the items that were lost on the way. In the same way, if anyone fails during *Pesach* to absorb its message in the fullest sense, the last day of *Pesach* provides another opportunity.

Since the word *Pesach* comes from the Hebrew to jump, indicating passing over our limitations, the theme of the holiday is service to God beyond limitations. Each day of the festival represents a higher jump over our limitations, until the last day, which is considered the highest jump of all.

ACHARON SHEL PESACH AND *MASHIACH*

The connection to *Mashiach* is what is especially unique about the eighth day of *Pesach*. We find that the *Haftorah* read on that day is about the predictions of Isaiah concerning the Messianic era. The Ba'al Shem Tov explained that every Jew experiences a glimmer of the light of *Mashiach* on *Acharon Shel Pesach*, a spiritual foretaste of the era of redemption, and he made it a custom to wash for a third meal and call it *"Mashiach's Se'udah."*[43] In later generations of the chasidic movement, further ramifications were revealed of the Ba'al Shem Tov's concept. Rabbi Menachem Mendel, the third Lubavitcher Rebbe, is quoted as saying that the term "last days" of *Pesach* means that what began on the first night of *Pesach* is completed on the last days, when God took us out of Egypt and redeemed us through *Moses*, the first redeemer. The last day of *Pesach* is the holiday of the *last* redemption, from the last exile, through *Mashiach*, who is the last redeemer.

43. *Sefer Hasichot* 5700, p. 75, *Sefer Hasichot* 5696, p. 140, and *Sefer Hasichot* 5703.

Rabbi Shalom Dovber, the fifth Rebbe of Lubavitch, introduced the custom of drinking four cups of wine during that meal, just as four cups are drunk at the *seder* on the first two nights. In 5666, he had the *Se'udah* of *Acharon Shel Pesach* with the students of the *yeshivah* he founded. He ordered that four cups of wine should be given to each student and said "This is *Mashiach's Se'udah*." It was understood that the teaching was not only for that year but for every year thereafter.

The reason for the custom also has some basis in non-mystical Torah sources. One might say that the four cups of the first days correspond to the four cups of retribution that God is going to make the nations drink in the future. Corresponding to them, God is going to give the Jewish People four cups of consolation.[44]

The connection of the future cups to *Pesach* can be understood according to the principle that at the Exodus from Egypt the channel was opened also for the future redemption. The earlier redemption made the later one possible, and it began a process leading to the later redemption. We drink the four cups of *Acharon Shel Pesach* at the end of the day at *Se'udat Mashiach* to elicit the revelation of the four cups of the future since all the revelations of the future depend on our service now.[45] The preparation does not only involve removing the obstacles that prevent the future revelation, which we accomplish by avoiding sin, but also drinking the four cups to elicit and draw down the revelations, the "four cups" of the future.[46]

---

44. *Talmud Yerushalmi, Pesachim*, beginning of ch. 10, *Bereishit Rabbah* 88:5.

45. *Tanya*, ch. 37.

46. *Likkutei Sichot*, vol. 4, p. 1299.

In addition to the meal and the four cups there is the custom of Rabbi Yosef Yitzchak, the sixth Rebbe of Lubavitch, called *Mashiach's* Dance, and this has two explanations:

1. Our trust that *Mashiach* will come quickly in our days inspires us to dance, and hence the dance is called "*Mashiach's* Dance."
2. During the dance there is a glimmer of *Mashiach*, along the lines of the Ba'al Shem Tov's teaching that there is generally a glimmer of *Mashiach* on this day. According to this, *Mashiach's* Dance means the dance in which *Mashiach* himself participates.

In connection with the Ba'al Shem Tov's statement that a revelation of the light of *Mashiach* shines at *Mashiach's Se'udah*, it should be noted that the Ba'al Shem Tov's teachings in general are related to the coming of *Mashiach*. In a famous letter, the Ba'al Shem Tov relates that he ascended to the chambers of *Mashiach*, where he heard "When will you come?" *Mashiach* responded, "when your wellsprings [of chasidism] are spread to the outside world."[47]

The reason for the custom of eating the physical meal is that the light of *Mashiach* that shines on that day should permeate the human body in the physical world. Whatever the person does throughout the coming year should be permeated with self-sacrifice, with the idea of serving God beyond limitations. As a result, the light of *Mashiach* and the *yechidah* become synonymous.

The reason the meal was introduced by the Ba'al Shem Tov and not by one of his predecessors is that as the darkness of exile

---

47. *Keter Shem Tov*, p. 3.

gets darker and darker, the strongest light is required to illumi-nate the darkness of the world. This reason relates to the nega-tive aspect of exile, but from another perspective, since we are getting closer and closer to redemption, we get to experience a foretaste of the Messianic era.

It is at *Mashiach's Se'udah* that the glimmer of *Mashiach* that every Jew experiences spiritually is also drawn down into physi-cality, for in general every spiritual matter needs to be linked to something physical if it is to have a permanent effect.

The connection of *Acharon Shel Pesach* and the light of *Mashiach* can also be appreciated in light of the principle explained in Jew-ish mysticism that all divine revelation constantly increases, so that it reaches its greatest intensity as it is about to conclude.[48] Therefore, since redemption and liberation are the major themes of the entire festival of *Pesach*, the idea of *Mashiach*, the ultimate redemption and liberation, is especially connected to the last day of *Pesach*.

There is another dimension of the connection of the last day with the coming of *Mashiach*.[49] Since biblically it is now no longer known as *Pesach*, it is only a holiday rabbinically, and in celebrat-ing the holiday we are bringing holiness to what is essentially a weekday. Thus, *Acharon Shel Pesach* is connected with human beings bringing Godliness to the mundane world. And this will be the greatness of the future redemption, Godliness revealed on even the lowest levels, as stated in the book of Isaiah, "And the glory of God will be revealed, and all flesh will see together that God has spoken."[50]

---

48. See *Siddur Admor Ha'emtz'ai, Derushei Seudat Shabbat*.

49. *Likkutei Sichot*, vol. 4, p. 1298.

50. Isaiah 40:5.

9

☙

Shavuot: Uniting the Spiritual and the Physical

"And you shall make a feast of weeks." (Deuteronomy 16:10)

The word *Shavuot* means weeks, referring to the fact that *Shavuot* occurs following the counting of seven complete weeks of *Sefirat Ha'omer*. Why, we might wonder, is this stressed to the point that it is the name of the whole holiday? In the previous chapter we discussed the process of refining the animal soul that a Jew undertakes during the counting of the *Omer*. This is the significance of the fact that the *Omer* offering was of barley, animal food. He must count the *Omer* for forty-nine days, eliciting the mystical "forty-nine gates of understanding" through his own efforts. At this point the animal soul has been refined to the greatest extent humanly possible, and it is impossible to proceed further based on human effort. In order to achieve the next stage, the "fiftieth gate" must be given as a divine gift on the fiftieth day. Even though a gift is something given and not earned, it nevertheless retains a connection to what the person achieved himself, as the Talmud comments, that one does not give someone a gift unless the recipient of the gift did something to benefit the giver.[1] This is the meaning of *Shavuot*: the spiritual elicitation that God grants after we have achieved as much as we can on our own.

The name "the time of the giving of the Torah" refers to a different, actually higher, dimension of the holiday of *Shavuot*, one that has nothing whatsoever to do with a Jew's individual efforts to refine himself. This dimension is experienced by the entire Jewish people collectively on the sixth of Sivan, the anniversary of the original giving of the Torah. When the Jewish calendar was calculated by the court in Jerusalem based on witnesses giving testimony concerning the new moon, it could happen that variations in the number of days in the months of *Iyar* and *Nissan* would lead to the fiftieth day of the counting of the *Omer,* and thus the holiday of *Shavuot,* falling on either the fifth or seventh of *Sivan.* Even now, when the calendar follows a fixed cycle, *Shavuot* can still fall on a day other than the sixth of *Sivan* for an individual crossing the International Dateline. Thus, the concept of *Shavuot,* is connected to the culmination of the counting of the *Omer,* the individual dimension of the holiday. This chapter will focus on the spiritual dimension of the giving of the Torah that reoccurs every *Shavuot* and which the Jews experience collectively.

---

1. As it is frequently quoted in chasidic philosophy. For example, see *Sefer Hama'amarim* 5666, p. 131; *Hodi'eini* 5705, ch. 20. See also *Gittin* 50b; *Bava Metzia* 16a.

THE REVELATION AT SINAI

The crucial event in Jewish history and, in fact, in the fulfillment of the world's destiny, is the revelation of Sinai. The details of the Torah's account convey the monumental nature of the event, but a number of the details require explanation. This event was, as the *Midrash* tells us, not only experienced by the entire Jewish nation that had left Egypt, but also by all Jewish souls that will ever exist—even the souls of converts were all present.[2] There was thunder and lightning, fire and smoke, and the sounding of the *shofar*; and each Jewish man, woman, and child was able to say that he or she had been addressed by God personally.[3] The *Midrash* also relates the puzzling detail that when God said the Ten Commandments the echo usually produced by a loud sound was absent. While all of these details may contribute to our sense of the momentousness of *Matan Torah*, it is still not clear exactly why the Torah had to be given in this manner.

The Talmud[4] relates that when God was about to give the Torah at Sinai, the angels complained to God, asking why beings of flesh and blood should be worthy of such a precious gift. God turned to Moses and asked him to answer them. Moses replied that the first commandment is, "I am the Lord Your God, Who took you out of Egypt"[5] and asked the angels if they ever descended to Egypt. He continued, "'Honor your father and mother'—do you have a father and a mother?" He then quoted other commandments, "You shall not steal, you shall not murder,[6]" etc., asking

---

2. *Shemot Rabbah* 28, 4.
3. *Yalkut Shimoni*, Exodus 20:2.
4. *Shabbat* 88b ff.
5. *Shemot* 20:2.
6. Ibid. 13.

the angels if they possessed an evil inclination. Of course, the angels could not answer him. Moses was victorious with his answer, and God gave the Torah on earth at Mount Sinai.

One might ask the following: Angels can only deal with spiritual concepts, so the Torah that the angels wanted was obviously a purely spiritual one. However, wasn't the Torah as studied on a spiritual level something the angels already possessed? What did the angels really want?

It is also unclear why God selected out of the 613 commandments the particular commandments that make up the Decalogue. Most of the Ten Commandments are basic to morality and appear logically necessary to any reasonable person. Even though the laws themselves were simple, their presentation by God with thunder and lightning and so forth indicates monumental emphasis. One would think that such circumstances would accompany the giving of mysterious, arcane laws in order to insure their observance. Why give *these* Ten Commandments in such a way? The question is even more pointed: Why was it necessary for God to give any commandments at all at Sinai, since all the laws were studied and observed from Abraham's time and passed on from generation to generation?[7] Actually, there was nothing new at all said at Mount Sinai.

Chasidic philosophy answers that it is not the actual laws that necessitated such an upheaval, but rather the Godly force within them that caused the world to tremble, thunder to sound, lightning to strike, and the *shofar* to blow. The laws themselves are comparable to a body, and the Godly force in the commandments is comparable to a soul. The intensity of the revelation represented a new dimension added to the "soul" of the commandments—the dimension of God's essence.

---

7. *Yoma* 28b, *Kiddushin* 82a.

Before Sinai both spirituality and physicality had their own boundaries and limitations. The relationship of the physical and spiritual was similar to that of a body and a soul: Although there is a strong relationship between the two, and one has an effect on the other, it is clear nevertheless that the spiritual and the physical remain discrete categories. Similarly, before Sinai, the physical world and spirituality influenced each other, but remained distinctly separate.

NULLIFYING THE DECREE

The *Midrash*[8] gives the following parable for the change that occurred at Sinai. There was a decree about two countries: "The people of Rome are not allowed to descend to Syria, and the people of Syria are not allowed to go up to Rome." Similarly, when God created the world, He decreed, "The heavens are God's heavens, but the earth He gave to the children of man."[9] When God gave the Torah, He nullified the decree[10] and said, "The ones below should elevate to the ones above and the ones above should descend, and I will be the first, as it is written, 'And God descended upon Mt. Sinai.'"[11]

God then descended at Mount Sinai and said to Moses, "Go up to God." Thus, at Sinai the decree was broken and supernal

---

8. *Tanchuma, Va'era* 15; *Shemot Rabbah* 12, 3.

9. Psalms 115:16.

10. The word decree in Hebrew—*gezeirah*—has also another meaning: cutting. The spiritual and the physical are opposites and were cut off from each other in two different planes.

11. *Shemot* 24:1.

beings could descend and earthly beings could ascend. God gave man the ability to transform the body and the world into something holy. The power given to man at Sinai, to transform the physical into the spiritual by observing the commandments, was the power to perform something that had been impossible. Each of the 613 commandments is connected to something physical. At the same time, each one is Godly. Therefore, after Sinai, when a Jew uses Godly power to transform the physical object into a holy entity—he does something contrary to logic. When one lights a candle before *Shabbat*, for instance, actual holiness inheres in the physical candle and the match used to light it.

HUMAN EFFORT

The linkage of the spiritual and the physical can come about through God revealing His power and glory in this world, or the initiation can come from the human beings to become one with God. Ultimately, however, God's intention in creating the world was that the initiation should be from below since something that comes from our own effort is much more permanent and inward; when it comes from above, it is only superficial since the nature of the world does not change. Sometimes a person can achieve a goal through his own efforts, but nevertheless there is some external factor that inspires him and provides the initial impetus. The divine intention for man's spiritual service, in contrast, is that it should be completely self-initiated, as in the case of a person who has independently determined that a certain goal should be striven for and who inspires himself, so to speak.

The ultimate goal is the complete union between the Godly and the physical. This was demonstrated by God at Sinai, but only so as to give us a head start, followed by our own efforts, beginning the day after Sinai. We were to take this ability to work to change ourselves and to transform the world around us and to become one with God. The intent, thus, was for our spiritual service to be the key element. God had the option of lifting us up to heaven and giving us the Torah there. He chose instead to come down to us, as we are in a body, so that now we must change ourselves and the world around us into a dwelling place for God.

The Godliness that comes from the intrinsic potential of human spiritual service is limited, and therefore it can not transform the physical into spiritual. Before *Matan Torah* what was revealed to the world was not God's essence, but only God's attributes, and therefore also limited. At Sinai, God revealed an essential connection to the Jewish people at Sinai, beyond any definition, even of his name. That is why it says in the opening statement of the decalogue "I . . . who took you out of Egypt." God is saying that He, the Infinite One revealed in Sinaitic revelation, is the same One who took the Jews out of Egypt.[12]

---

12. It is also interesting to note that, as the *Midrash* points out, the first word of the Ten Commandments, *Anochi*, is an Egyptian word (*Tanchuma, Yitro* 36 [Buber ed.], *Yalkut Shimoni,* Exodus 20:2). One would think that the first word would be in Hebrew, especially since it refers to God Himself. The explanation is that Egypt, at that time, was the paradigm of all corruption. The purpose of Sinaitic revelation is to transform even the lowest level of existence and to unite it with God Himself, and God refers to Himself in Egyptian to demonstrate this point.

The opening sentence of the Ten Commandments begins with the word "I" and continues with God's name and then the word *Elokecha,* (your God)—a Hebrew word. The normal word for "I" is *Ani*; however, the word *Anochi* means, "Only I know who I am," that is, "Only I know my greatness," and that cannot be defined by any name of God, for the essence of God has no definition. God revealed Himself at Sinai for the first time as His true essence, which is beyond names. Therefore He gave

We can now answer the question about why the angels objected to the giving of the Torah to mortals. They realized that the Torah that the Jewish people were to be given was not simply spiritual, but one with God's essence, and this was what they wanted. Moses convinced the angels that the only reason the Jews were to receive such a gift was that it takes the essence of God to transform the physical into spiritual and the evil inclination—the *yeitzer hara*—into the good inclination—the *yeitzer tov*. This is also the reason God chose the simple commandments: to demonstrate that even basic acts of morality, when observed simply because God so commanded, unite a person with God.

We can also answer some of our other initial questions. The explanation of the absence of an echo at *Matan Torah* is that an echo is sound bouncing off some object. At Sinai, the Ten commandments were *absorbed* by the world, preparing the world so that man's fulfillment of *mitzvot* with physical objects can transform the world into a holy place.

Although in some chasidic literature it seems that the purpose of the thunder and lightning was to effect a feeling of humility

---

simple commandments, for the greater one is, the lower one can descend. The simplicity of the commandments demonstrated the greatness of their origin.

Accordingly, chasidic philosophy answers the question of why God says in the first commandment, "I am the Lord, Your God, who took you out of Egypt from the house of bondage." If God wants to identify Himself, He can mention much more than taking the Jews out of Egypt: He created the world *ex nihilo*, which is much greater than defying nature by sending the ten plagues or splitting the Red Sea. The word for Egypt in Hebrew, however, is *Mitzraim* and it is related to the word *meitzarim*, which means "limitations." God's revelation of His essence at Sinai gave us the potential to transcend all limitations.

and subservience in the Jewish people, chasidic philosophy ultimately concludes that if that would have been the only purpose
then the revelation of God should have been enough. On the
contrary, the trembling induced by thunder and lightning pertains
merely to the body, but the revelation of God produced a complete subservience in the most profound levels of the Jewish soul.
Nevertheless, the trembling of the earth was actually an expression of the comprehensive transformation that was occurring to
all existence at the time of *Matan Torah*, revealing that God is
the only true existence.[13]

THE SPIRITUAL SERVICE OF THE PATRIARCHS

Our great forefathers and foremothers, who were supremely holy,
could not bring about the change in the physical world that we
have been discussing by their performance of *mitzvot*. Their own
observance was strictly between their souls and God since a finite being, no matter how holy, is still limited and therefore cannot do the impossible.

Chasidic philosophy explains that the spiritual service of the
Patriarchs *did* have some effect on the physical world, as is indicated by the principle that the spiritual service of the Jewish
people (which is able to transform the physical) is a continuation
of that of the Patriarchs.[14] They served God with their souls,
through meditation, love, and devotion. Since they had such lofty
souls, their bodies were automatically attuned to respond to their

---

13. *Likkutei Sichot*, vol. 33 , p. 24.

14. In Hebrew, *Ma'aseh Avot siman lebanim*. See Ramban, Genesis
12:6; *Tanchuma, Lech Lecha*.

soul's feelings. Everything that they did with their bodies or the world was merely an expression of their spiritual life, analogous to a person who is happy and who automatically responds to that inner happiness physically, by looking happy. In the same way, as the Patriarchs served God with their souls, their physical demeanor responded accordingly.

Nevertheless, their bodies, no matter how much they sanctified them, were merely vehicles through which the soul could express itself.[15] After Sinai, as we have been saying, the whole emphasis has been to *transform* the physical—our home, our business—and to make it holy. The soul's purpose is to transform the physical world.

THE CHOSEN PEOPLE

Another important change in the Jewish people's existence that took place at *Matan Torah* involves the very nature of their closeness to God. Starting with *Matan Torah*, the Jewish people ac-

---

15. Their service, involving physical objects, was nevertheless a necessary preparation to the giving of the Torah and the service of transforming the physical into the spiritual. This explains why God waited 2000 years before giving the Torah. Everything that happened before Sinai was meant to prepare the world by elevating the human soul to its maximum. The Patriarchs were only able to elevate themselves to the root of created beings. Once we elevated ourselves to the highest point a finite being can attain, it was then time to receive the Torah. Then, God gave us something that we would never achieve on our own, and since then there has been no limit to the elevation that the Jewish people have been able to achieve.

quired the status of having been *chosen*[16] in addition to their prior status as God's children. The significance of God's choice can be understood by considering human choice as an analogy. When someone has a natural disposition to love something, that love is limited. The person's nature confers a particular definition to his character traits, dispositions, and abilities. Since these influence his affections, the strength of a natural attachment to something is also bounded and given a certain character by his nature.

True choice, by contrast, derives from a person's essence. The reason is that true choice does not derive from any reason or rationale but only from a person's free will unbounded by any natural inclination compelling the choice. We can illustrate this by noting that a person can choose something that utterly clashes with his natural inclinations and that desire for something due to pure choice has greater strength, therefore, than desire motivated by natural inclination.

The same thing is true, so to speak, with respect to God. God's love and desire for the Jews, which derives from the Jews' status as children, is analogous to the natural love of a father for a child, a connection that relates to a particular aspect of the personality. At *Matan Torah*, by contrast, God *chose* the Jewish people, and choice is an expression of the chooser's essence, transcending any particular form or definition.

This elevation of God's attachment to the Jewish people produced a corresponding change in the Jews' devotion to God, which from then on also derived not from *their* natural inclinations, but

---

16. See *Magen Avraham* 60b. See also *Shulchan Aruch Harav* 60, 4: When saying *"ubanu becharta"* one should have in mind the giving of the Torah.

from their essence. This changed their spiritual service from that of a child to that of a servant.

The distinction between a child and a servant as categories of serving God is an important concept in chasidic philosophy.[17] The service of a child for a parent derives from the natural inclination of a child to love his father and to be in awe of him. Similarly the spiritual service of those who are called "children" derives from a natural trait of love and fear of God, and therefore their service can hardly be called service at all since such a person is simply doing what he is inclined to do. In contrast, the service of a servant is contrary to his nature, and when he expresses the devotion of a true servant whose whole existence is to serve the master, he completely nullifies his own ego and subordinates it to the master's needs.[18]

GOD, THE TORAH, AND THE JEWISH PEOPLE

The ramifications of the change that occurred at the giving of the Torah on Mount Sinai can ultimately be detailed with reference to God, the Giver of the Torah, the Jewish people, and the Torah itself.[19]

1. As far as God is concerned, the Torah states that God wrote Himself into the Torah. The first word in the Ten Commandments is *Anochi*, which, the Talmud explains,[20] can be read as an acronym for *Ana Nafshi ketavit yehavit*—"I

---

17. See *Sefer Hama'amarim 5666, p. 308 ff.*
18. *Likkutei Sichot*, vol. 11, p. 4 ff.
19. *Sefer Hama'amarim Melukat*, vol. 4, p. 275.
20. *Shabbat* 105a, according to the text of *Ein Yaakov*.

wrote and gave Myself." I, in this case, refers to God's essence, so that the above statement means I gave myself away in the Torah.

2. As far as the Jew is concerned, the major change stems from the Torah being given on earth, in that he has proprietorship, so to speak, over the Torah. This means that the authority to determine *halachah* is in the possession of human beings. This is illustrated by the famous incident in the Talmud in which Rabbi Eliezer ben Hyrcanos disagrees with the majority of the Sages on a certain halachic point. Even though a heavenly voice declares Rabbi Eliezer's opinion to be the correct one, the view of the majority prevails, and afterwards it is revealed that at the time, God was laughing and saying "My children have defeated Me!"[21] After *Matan Torah*, the Jewish people have had the ability to influence the physical world, and the physical world reacts according to how the Jewish court decides through the study of Torah. This ability derives from God's essence, and after *Matan Torah* it was incorporated into the essence of the Jewish people.

3. Concerning the Torah, from *Matan Torah* on, the *mitzvot* of the Torah have had the power to influence and change the very makeup and nature of the person in the physical world so that they should conform to the commandments of the Torah. Thus, the commandment "You shall not kill" is both a command and a promise (i.e., the inner nature of the person is such that he will not kill).[22] This is true, in

---

21. *Bava Metzia* 59b.

22. *Likkutei Torah, Bamidbar* 13:3. If a person does kill, he is going against his inner nature.

fact, of all the commandments of the Torah. This is why it was necessary to gather all the Jewish souls that will ever live at the revelation of Sinai, for with the uttering of the Decalogue the Jews were not learning things that they would not have known otherwise, but experiencing a change in their very nature.

This difference between the service of the Patriarchs and the service after *Matan Torah* is indicated in our Sages' comment on the verse, "For fragrance your oils are good, oil poured forth is your name."[23] Our Sages comment,[24] "All the songs that the patriarchs said before You were scents, however regarding us, 'oil poured forth is your name.'"

This comment illuminates the above-discussed three aspects of the change that took place after *Matan Torah*. The basic difference between scent and oil, that scent is merely the diffusion of the fragrant oil, is relevant to the change in the Giver of the Torah. The Torah in its own right, God's wisdom, is merely an expression of God. After *Matan Torah*, however, God's essence (symbolized by oil) was united with the Torah. Thus, this also applies to the Torah itself, that it was united with God's essence.

A further difference between oil and scent is that when one smells fragrant oil, nothing is thereby removed from it. However, when one takes some of the oil itself, then there is less of it in its original place. This corresponds to the fact that when the Torah was given below, the ability to determine the *halachah* was taken from the spiritual realm.

---

23. *Shir Hashirim* 1:3.
24. *Shir Hashirim Rabbah*, 1:3.

Yet another difference between oil and scent is that scent gradually dissipates until there is nothing left of it, and then the benefit from it stops. Something edible, however (such as oil), remains in the person's body after he eats it, even though it is transformed to flesh and blood, and it affects the person's attributes so that they reflect the qualities of the food. In reference to *mitzvot*, this refers to the spiritual effect of fulfilling *mitzvot*, and all the more so, learning Torah.

The service of the Patriarchs did not have a permanent effect on the world; however, the learning of Torah and especially the fulfillment of *mitzvot* after *Matan Torah* creates a change in the world inwardly and permanently.

Since God is above time and the revelation of His Torah that occurred at *Matan Torah* is also above time, *Matan Torah* is actually something that is presently and always occurring. On the phrase "which I command you today" in the *Shema*,[25] Rashi comments, "that they should be new to you as though you heard them this day." How can a human being feel that something that happened thousands of years ago is something that is happening today? The answer is that every Jew possesses levels of the soul that are not limited to the body and the realm of time and space. If he can only tap into these levels, he can experience the crucial event of the giving of the Torah, not as something that happened thousands of years ago, but as something truly new.

---

25. Deuteronomy 11:13; see also Deuteronomy 6:6, Rashi.

10

Shabbat:
A New World

"And God blessed the seventh day and made it holy, for on it He rested from all His work. . . ."   (Genesis 2:3)

Shabbat is the heart of the Jewish religion, as indicated by the Talmud's statement that observing *Shabbat* is equivalent to observing the whole Torah.[1] *Shabbat* is man's link to the infinite and to his own soul, enabling him to transcend time and space. The weekday prayers are considered to be the *Shabbat* of the day, so that every day there is a radiance of *Shabbat*, which elevates all the Torah and *mitzvot* of that day. On *Shabbat* itself, the soul expresses itself in its pristine essence.

---

1. *Berachot* 1:5; *Nedarim* end of ch. 3; *Shemot Rabbah* 25, 16; *Zohar* II 89a.

The Torah states that man observes *Shabbat* because God rested from all His work on the seventh day of creation.[2] This raises several questions: The *Mishnah* indicates[3] that God created the world through "utterances" such as "Let there be light."[4] If so, how can speaking be considered work for the infinite God when it is not so considered even for human beings? The *Midrash*, as a matter of fact, states explicitly that God's creation of the world should not be considered literal work.[5] The concept of work on *Shabbat* does not conform, evidently, to the familiar concept of work.[6]

RESTING FROM CREATION

As we have already explored, the Ba'al Shem Tov explains that the world is constantly dependent for its very existence on God's initial act of creation.[7] God is the only being who exists inde-

---

2. Genesis 2:2.

3. *Avot* 5:1.

4. Genesis 3:1.

5. *Bereishit Rabbah* 3, 2; 10, 2.

6. We might also wonder why there is no prohibition of speaking on *Shabbat*. If God rested from creating the world through "utterances," then we should be especially prohibited from performing the same action, yet this is not the case in the laws of *Shabbat*. There is no Biblically-based prohibition of speech on *Shabbat*, although some forms of speech are forbidden by the Rabbis in order to emphasize that on *Shabbat* a Jew is not supposed to concern himself with weekday affairs. The answer is that there is a major difference between man's speech, and God's, which is the medium for creation, unlike man's. Consequently, only our actions parallel God's words, which God ceased to use on *Shabbat*. However, some words resemble action in that words can influence action; therefore, it was decreed Rabbinically that there should be restraint in certain kinds of speech on *Shabbat* (*Likkutei Torah, Torat Shmuel* 5630 "*Avot Melachot*").

7. See *Tanya, Sha'ar Hayichud Veha'emunah*, ch. 1.

pendently, and every other existence depends on His existence.[8] Therefore the world must be created constantly, remaining dependent on divine creative force. This raises an interesting question about *Shabbat*: How can we say that God rested from all His work on the seventh day, when the world cannot exist for one second without God's agency? Moreover, according to Jewish mysticism, the commemoration of an event always involves a recurrence of that event spiritually. Thus, there is an Exodus from Egypt on every *Pesach* and this question applies to every *Shabbat*.[9] Many commentaries explain the Torah's statement that God rested on *Shabbat* in the sense of not creating any *new* creations, so that God was still creating the world. However, this doesn't seem to be the literal translation of the scriptural wording, which indicates that God rested on the seventh day from the work He had already done.

The command to man to rest in commemoration of God's resting also requires explanation: If the idea is to periodically renew one's awareness of the Creator and commemorate His creation of the world, why do we focus on God's resting from creation, the cessation of the creative process?

Further, most of the activities that the Torah classifies as work are not particularly strenuous, while many strenuous activities are technically permissible on *Shabbat*, and this also begs explanation.

If the quintessential theme of *Shabbat* is rest, then we might also wonder why we are commanded to have delight on *Shabbat*.[10] What is the connection of delight to rest?

---

8. *Hilchot Yesodei Hatorah* 1:3

9. Our rest parallels divine rest according to the principle that we have explored that all events in the physical realm parallel events in the spiritual realm.

10. See *Shulchan Aruch, Orach Chayim* 242.

However, as we will further explore, according to chasidic philosophy, a change in the world's basic existence occurs on *Shabbat*, the deeper meaning of the cessation of God's creation of the world through utterances. The concept of divine speech is, of course, not to be taken literally, since God has no physical attributes. All expressions attributing physical actions to God such as speaking or physical states such as pleasure or anger are merely metaphors, since the Torah speaks in the language of man. What, then, is divine speech?

To explain by analogy, a person communicates his thoughts and ideas to another through speech. When a person is simply thinking, he is alone, so to speak, with his thoughts; nothing else exists. When he speaks, he immediately acknowledges the presence of someone other than himself. Communication thus involves a departure from the self, going out of oneself.

In the same way, when we speak of God on the level of divine thought, as He exists to Himself, we refer to the true awareness that He alone is the only existence. However, on such a level the world could never exist normally, for the natural state of the world creates the appearance of independent existence.

The only way to create a seemingly autonomous world is for God to conceal his divine self-awareness. He must conceal His light and lower Himself to permit a feeling of self in man, a process described in Jewish mysticism as *tzimtzum*, or condensation. This resembles speech, which is simultaneously revelation and concealment. To the listener, speech is purely revelation through which the ideas of the speaker become known. For the speaker, however, speech is concealment, since whenever a person speaks, he conceals more than he reveals.[11]

_____

11. God's communication with prophets is also called "speech" for this reason. A Godly "thought" is too lofty for a human being to grasp, so

When a person communicates with another, only a fraction is expressed, of his feelings, or of an idea as it exists mentally. Most of it is restrained, or held back, because thoughts and feelings originate from a realm that transcends the verbal and that can only partially be revealed through words. As a matter of fact, the limiting and focusing of thought is a pre-condition for communication.

The same process takes place on a higher spiritual level. The human personality is described in Jewish mysticism as having exactly ten primary faculties: three intellectual ones and seven emotional ones. This parallels the ten divine attributes through which God manifests Himself. During the week, the world's existence is based on God's emotions, and just as we find in man, the emotions are directed outside the self. Intellect, by contrast, is totally for the self.

Strictly speaking, divine intellect is actually also used throughout the week for creation, although it is not objective intellect (the primary form of intellect, which is unconcerned with application), but intellect to stimulate emotions—just as in a human being there is objective and subjective intellect. Subjective intellect, the lower of the two levels, is the understanding of how a concept relates to the individual, as when one asks, "Does this have good or bad consequences?" In the same way, during the week, the main spiritual force revealed to the world derives from the seven divine emotions, whereas the three forces of intellect are limited and only operate in creation to evoke God's emotions.[12] We can de-

---

it must undergo limitation and concealment in order to reach a form that the prophet can receive and transmit to others.

12. This is the process by which the emotions are activated, generally speaking, in a human being: The intellect contemplates something that has certain emotional implications or associations, and the corresponding emotion is then summoned forth and enabled to function openly.

scribe this as objective intellect condensing itself for subjective thinking. On *Shabbat*, as we will explain, divine intellect radiates into the world in its pristine state.

The descent of divine objective intellect to the subjective level parallels other types of descent connected to work. In any type of work, labor, drawing, painting, building, etc., a person essentially has to lower himself from his general personality that is capable of a seemingly unlimited variety of activities and that is not confined to anything specific.[13]

This departure from or descent in the true self corresponds to the divine process of *tzimtzum* through which God condenses and limits Himself to maintain and interact with creation.

Work is associated conventionally with fatigue, being tired. A person becomes tired during the day because the nature of the soul is to be self-concerned. Strain and exertion result when the individual has to lower himself to deal with the physical world and not be himself, so to speak. Similarly, pure objective intellect experiences strain when it has to relate to the emotions since intellect naturally tends towards objectivity, understanding ideas independently of their emotional implications. Rest, then, is the reentry of the faculties and character traits into the

---

13. Moreoever, the activity of writing itself, for example, is specific and limited compared from where it originates in the intellect (e.g., when a person writes down an idea the intellect in general is not limited to the specific idea being written. When he does the actual writing, he thus descends from the limitlessness of possibility to the limitation of the specific). Another example of this descent is in the power of movement. When a person engages, for example, in construction, the source of his strength is not limited to anything specific, comparable to strength in its spiritual source. Moreover, spiritual strength is undifferentiated and on a higher level than actual strength.

self, a reconstitution of selfhood. This resembles the return of a worker from his workplace to his home, where his essential self is expressed, since at home he can pursue his true interests without the need to conform to the expectations of the workplace.

On the divine level, the *Shabbat* return of the method of speech to its source, so that God creates the world through divine thought, is God's "rest." Chasidic philosophy notes that when the three letters of the word *Shabbat*—*shin, bet,* and *tov*— are reversed, they spell the word "*tasheiv*," which is a derivative of the word return, alluding to the return of divine speech to its source and the world's subsequent experience of a higher and completely different life-force. This is the spiritual essence of *Shabbat.*

On the human level, paralleling the Divine, a Jew also returns to his essence. Chasidic philosophy, and Jewish mysticism in general, describes existence in terms of a hierarchy of spiritual levels, called "worlds." The lowest of these levels, the world of *Asiyah* (action), also comprises a physical level, our mundane physical world. Each level has its source in the level immediately above it, and each level is elevated and returns to its source on *Shabbat*, functioning on a higher level relative to its particular normal level.[14]

---

14. This elevation takes place not only in the loftiest spiritual levels, but on the lowly physical level, and there is a general absence of all evil. This is demonstrated by the Jerusalem Talmud's statement (*Demai* 4:1) that even an *am ha'aretz*—a boorish person—is incapable of lying on *Shabbat*, i.e., mundane reality has been altered so that it is against such a person's very nature to lie. The souls that are undergoing purification in *Gehinom*—Purgatory—also experience a reprieve from their suffering.

TWO DOMAINS

The mystical concept of the elevation associated with *Shabbat* can be found in metaphorical terms in the *Midrash*,[15] which relates that a heretic asked Rabbi Akiva that if God Himself observes *Shabbat*, then why does He violate His own laws by causing rain to fall (watering vegetation), wind to blow (carrying from one domain to another), grass to grow, and so forth? Rabbi Akiva answered that the labor of transferring from one domain to another provides an illustration. Since the whole world is God's private domain, then He does not violate the law of transferring from a private domain—*reshut hayachid*—to a public one—*reshut harabim*. Rabbi Akiva's response is at first puzzling because it does not answer the part of the question that relates to prohibited agricultural labors. However, since work on *Shabbat* involves a transfer from the level of thought to speech, then *all* prohibited labor on *Shabbat* exemplifies the labor of transfer from a private domain to a public one. This *Midrash*, then, teaches us a key concept concerning the prohibited labors of *Shabbat*. A private domain is subject to the control of an individual as opposed to many people, and this corresponds to the world's receiving its life-force on *Shabbat* from the level of divine thought on *Shabbat*, where all that exists is divine unity. If a Jew performs a *malachah*—a prohibited labor—then he removes the world from a private domain, as it exists in divine thought, to the public domain of the world as derived from divine speech.

The spiritual service of *Shabbat,* which is to meditate on God's unity, has the same theme. Thus, transferring from one domain to another constitutes a denial that all of existence is really God's

---

15. *Bereishit Rabbah* 11, 5; *Shemot Rabbah* 30, 9.

private domain, that God is ultimately the only existence. The world is created in a way that it is possible to err and think that there are two domains, one of holiness and one of evil and impurity. Rabbi Akiva's answer, thus, also refers to human awareness: By refraining from prohibited labor, a Jew establishes faith and knowledge of the truth that all existence is actually a private domain (literally "domain of a *yachid*—individual," and referring here to the *Yechido shel olam*—the one God of the world) and performing prohibited labor interrupts this awareness.[16] We can now understand why Shabbat commemorates God's resting specifically: When the world experiences a return to its source, then we achieve a renewed awareness that there is a source.

On *Shabbat*, then, there is revelation of divine unity, a removal of concealment. We also find in the Torah's description of divine rest from creation that the phrase, *Vayichal Elokim*—God completed His work, refers to God by the name *Elokim*, which indicates concealment. Chasidic philosophy interprets this phrase as "[That which is signified by the divine name] *Elokim* [i.e, concealment] ceased," which means that God's light shines through openly on *Shabbat*.

It is interesting to note that one of the explanations that Chasidic philosophy gives[17] for the prohibition of work on *Shabbat* is that God is then revealed to the world to a greater degree than during the week. It is thus disrespectful to do anything else but acknowledge the presence of the King. By contrast, God conceals Himself, so to speak, from us during the week by using the method of speech, and work is not considered disrespectful then. As a matter of fact, human work is necessary for the maintenance of

---

16. *Likkutei Sichot*, vol. 11, p. 68.
17. *Sefer Hama'amarim* 5666, p. 22.

God's creation of the world. Since it is not the normal custom of a King to be involved in mundane matters, and since, as we have seen, the creation of the world as a seemingly independent entity is a descent and self-limitation for God, we must elicit God's bestowal of creative force. This elicitation is through human labor during the week when it conforms to God's commandments (for example, if a businessman conducts his business honestly).

REFINING THE WORLD

Chasidic philosophy also explains the prohibition of work, activity leading to *tzimtzum*, in terms of man's spiritual service, whose goal is to refine and elevate the world. The purpose of involving oneself in the mundane activities is to purify and elevate the world by sifting through the good and the evil. Since everything is created by God, everything inevitably contains a spark of sanctity. Evil is defined in Jewish mysticism as the concealment of this sanctity, and hence of God's existence as revealed in the world. For this reason the entities of the spiritual realm that correspond to evil in the world are known as *kelipot*, which means shells. Just as a shell conceals the fruit that it covers, a *kelipah* conceals Godliness. Sifting, then, consists of using every part of the mundane world to serve God and revealing the sanctity contained within all creation.

For example, when one eats and uses the strength gained for learning Torah or performing *mitzvot*, ultimately the food is elevated by becoming a means to fulfill a divine purpose. Since, on *Shabbat*, certain levels of impurity are automatically dissolved, the objective is *not* for the individual to lower himself to sift, for there is no evil. The requisite activity is elevating good to even higher good. That is why it is prohibited to spend time sifting, which is also a form of descent: lowering oneself to deal with the negative and separate it from the positive.

When a Jew does any of the thirty-nine prohibited kinds of work, that activity also constitutes a descent in that it causes the life-force of the world to descend and become condensed, which constitutes work for God, since the spiritual and the earthly parallel each other.

In light of the above, the definition of work prohibited to a Jew on *Shabbat* becomes clear. Work is not to be understood as man's labor, but rather human action that causes *God* to labor (i.e., to undergo descent and *tzimtzum*). The thirty-nine prohibitions of work cause a new descent in the energy of the world that returned on Shabbat to its source, speech elevating to thought, from subjective intellect to objective intellect, and so forth.

That is why even building the Tabernacle is forbidden on *Shabbat,* for the whole purpose of the construction of the Tabernacle, and later the Temple, was to bring down "energy" from the spiritual realm down to earth and to enable man to ultimately elevate the world. Since on *Shabbat* everything returns to its source, it is not the proper time to cause God to descend.

One might wonder why sacrifices were nevertheless offered even on *Shabbat;* however, sacrifices and *Shabbat* are conceptually equivalent. Sacrifices essentially elevate the animal to God and the animalistic soul in us, returning them to their source, as opposed to causing the descent of Godliness into the world.

THE DELIGHT OF *SHABBAT*

Up to this point we have been considering the concept of rest on *Shabbat,* the return of the divine creative force to its source. However, *Shabbat* possesses a second dimension: The completion of all God's creations causes delight, since the return of everything back to its source indicates that the divine purpose has been accomplished. In the same vein, man is commanded to rest and also to do things that bring delight, such as enjoying *Shabbat* to the fullest, with good food, wine, etc.

The two distinctive time periods of *Shabbat* are conceptually significant. Friday night, the evening of *Shabbat*, is the return of the divine creative energies to their source, the idea of rest. On Friday night God feels delight in response to the completion of His work. On Saturday, however, God feels a higher delight.

We can explain by analogy that before a person actually has his house built, he derives a certain delight from his planning. Throughout the construction this pleasure is concealed and when the house is completed, the original pleasure of the anticipated completion becomes revealed with the completed house serving as its object. This pleasure can be likened to Friday night.

On *Shabbat* day, to continue the metaphor, there is a greater delight as the actual completion of the physical house leads to even more pleasure than that mentally anticipated by the builder. For example, when a person moves into the house, his delight is much greater than both the delight of the planning and that of contemplating the completed house. His delight comes from the fulfillment of his ultimate purpose, which is to live in the house and express his essential selfhood there. This delight is no longer directly connected to the house at all, but rather *ta'anug atzmi*— delight connected to the essential self.

According to Genesis 2:2, God "finished on the seventh day from the work he had done." The rabbis ask, didn't He finish on the sixth, as implied by resting on the seventh? One of the answers is that God did create something on *Shabbat*—rest itself. As the *Midrash* says, "What was the world missing? The idea of rest, therefore on *Shabbat* came rest and through that all His work was complete."

Rest is not an entity in itself that can be created, we might object, but rather the abstention from work. Why was the world missing rest, and why was it necessary to create rest when it automatically follows the cessation of work?

The concept of rest as a *Shabbat* creation, however, is not the tranquility of refraining from work, but rather inner spiritual peace related to inner essence, *ta'anug atzmi.* Connection with its essence is not something the world has on its own, so it can only come as a divine gift.

Again, *Shabbat* has two aspects: The first is rest following the six days of labor. Then there is a higher aspect of Shabbat that is beyond time, unrelated to the six days of weekday activity, corresponding to the delight and pleasure God receives from His creations, which is unrelated to the six days of labor. On this level *Shabbat* should no longer be considered a seventh day, which implies continuity with the six preceding days. After *Shabbat* the whole cycle of time begins again, after being suspended on the seventh day, and accordingly we can understand *chasidic* philosophy's explanation of why the number of days continuously returns to the first day (i.e., each Sunday is a new first day), not an eighth day or a fifteenth day, and so forth, as would be the case if the days were simply numbered consecutively throughout the year.

On the human level the same two aspects apply, but here there seems to be a paradox. We are commanded to prepare for the *Shabbat*—we *make* the Shabbat happen. At the same time, Shabbat is called God's great gift.[18] The definition of a gift, however, is something unearned.

---

18. *Shabbat* 10b, *Zohar* III 122b.

Our identification of two distinct phases of *Shabbat*, however, allows us to resolve the paradox as follows: The initial delight of *Shabbat* is based on how much one prepares oneself for the *Shabbat*.[19] Afterward, however, a delight becomes manifest that is even greater than the delight that results from the accomplishment of work.

Corresponding, then, to God's delight in the accomplishment of His work, man also experiences delight from the completion of his spiritual labor on Friday night. On Saturday he receives a higher delight in the form of a gift, something not commensurate with his spiritual service, corresponding to God's *ta'anug atzmi*. On Friday each level of creation returns to its source, as we have seen, in the level immediately above it, and accordingly, each level, including the soul of a Jew, feels *bitul*, a sense of subservience and a sense of ceasing to exist as a separate entity as self awareness becomes subsumed in awareness of a higher reality. This level, called *bitul hayesh*, however, is not complete because it is still possible to speak of an *individual* who feels a sense of self-nullification. The human response to divine delight on Saturday, the delight of essence, is *bitul hametziut*, a level at which it is no longer possible to speak of an individual who feels self-nullification; awareness of Divinity is all. A well-known concept in Judaism is the extra soul, which one receives on *Shabbat*.[20] The person's loss of this extra soul as *Shabbat* ends makes him feel faint, and this is the reason for smelling spices during the *havdalah* ceremony marking the conclusion of *Shabbat*.

---

19. This accords with the statement of our sages that "He who exerts effort before *Shabbat* can eat on *Shabbat*" (*Avodah Zarah* 3a). This statement, according to chasidic philosophy, also alludes to the spiritual influence of the preceding six days on the following *Shabbat*.

20. *Beitza* 16a.

We are now in a position to understand the deeper meaning of the extra soul, which corresponds to the achievement of the level of *bitul hametziut*. We can also answer our earlier question concerning why man is commanded to experience delight on *Shabbat* and its connection to rest. A person's experience of the higher level of pleasure on *Shabbat* is necessary to elicit and draw down the maintenance of the world's existence from the divine level of thought, which, as we explained earlier, is the true meaning of God's resting, the elevation of each level of existence to its source.

SHABBAT AND REDEMPTION

An interesting apparent contradiction occurs between the Babylonian and the Jerusalem Talmud. The Babylonian Talmud states that if the Jewish people were to observe *Shabbat* twice, then the messianic redemption would occur.[21] The Jerusalem Talmud makes the same statement except that it only refers to one *Shabbat*.[22] Chasidic philosophy reveals, however, that there is actually no contradiction. The *Zohar*[23] speaks of two levels of *Shabbat* observance, and, according to chasidic philosophy, this is the referrant of the "two Sabbaths" mentioned in the Babylonian Talmud, so that both Talmuds actually speak of one literal *Shabbat*. Thus, the Jewish people's achievement of the second level, in which all existence ceases to have any independent existence apart from God, brings and essentially constitutes the messianic

---

21. *Shabbat* 112b.
22. *Ta'anit* 5:1.
23. I 5b.

redemption, a state in which Divinity is perceived as the true reality.

The world is then returned to its original state in which the divine presence is openly revealed, the ultimate implication of *Shabbat* as return.

11

ว่า

Yom Tov:
The Joy of Understanding

"And you shall rejoice on your holiday." (Deuteronomy 16:14)

We have already discussed that on every *Yom Tov* there is a spiritual reoccurrence of the original event being commemorated and the light of the original divine revelation shines once more. In this chapter we will discuss some of the other aspects that apply to all *Yamim Tovim*.

An obvious way to approach the subject of *Yom Tov* is through a comparison between *Yom Tov* and *Shabbat*.

JOY AND DELIGHT

We have a commandment to celebrate *Shabbat* with delight[1] (*oneg*) whereas on *Yom Tov* there is also a commandment con-

---

1. Isaiah 58:13; *Shulchan Aruch, Orach Chaim* 243.

cerning *oneg*, but there is a direct biblical commandment, not pertaining to *Shabbat*, to celebrate with joy (*simchah*).[2] The obligation is to rejoice by drinking wine. Thus, the main stress is *oneg* on Shabbat and *simchah* on *Tom Tov*.

Joy and delight are two opposite phenomena. Delight is inward, hidden and concealed, and change cannot be discerned in a person's face when he is experiencing it. In contrast, the nature of joy is that when a person is in a joyful state, it is demonstrated in a physical way, such as bursting out in words, song, laughter and dance. In short, joy thrusts outward in obvious behavior.

Joy is particularly associated with understanding a concept, and the main spiritual service of *Yom Tov* is meditating on God's greatness. *Yom Tov* is a propitious time when a Jew is granted a special ability to achieve understanding as a result of his meditation. The fact that wine is associated with *simchah* is also significant in this respect. Wine, which has taste (in Hebrew the word *ta'am* means both taste and reason), represents the pleasure of understanding.[3]

Another dimension of joy is that it is usually derived from something out of the ordinary, such as a poor man suddenly becoming rich, or a prisoner unexpectedly being freed from prison, etc. In the same way, since *Yom Tov* usually occurs during the week, a weekday acquires an out-of-the ordinary degree of holiness, producing joy. *Shabbat*, by contrast, is always a holy day, and it therefore does not involve a radical change from the usual.

---

2. Deuteronomy 16:14. See *Shulchan Aruch, Orach Chaim* 529.

3. *Likkutei Torah, Derushim LeSukkot*, "*Ushe'avtem mayim*," p. 79d ff. See the section on *Simchat Beit Hasho'eivah* in the chapter on Sukkot.

These two contrasting emotions of delight and joy that a Jew feels on *Shabbat* and *Yom Tov* respectively are reflections of what is occurring on the spiritual level. Delight is much deeper and closer to the essence of God than joy is, and therefore the energy of *Shabbat* is loftier and more inward than on *Yom Tov*. Similarly, the faculty of delight in a human being stems from the innermost part of the soul. As a result of the spiritual revelation corresponding to delight on *Shabbat* there is a complete absence of spiritual impurity on *Shabbat*.

On *Yom Tov*, by contrast, where the theme is the light of joy, the light is not powerful enough to affect the darkness to that extent. Joy is more external, and the reason that it bursts outward is that its source is also more from the external dimension of the soul, not from the soul's essence.

What does it mean to say that God's light shines as an expression of joy? The tendency of joy is that it "breaks through boundaries,"[4] and there is less and less concealment. We find in human nature that when a person is joyously overwhelmed, for example at the wedding of an only child, the joy is boundless, and one can even be benevolent to one's enemy. So, too, on the day of *Yom Tov*, when God's delight is expressed in joy, the normal order of things is overturned and all concealment of Godliness is removed. One is in the presence of God. Moreover, when we meditate on God's greatness and achieve an understanding of it, which results in rejoicing, then God and the Jewish people can be said to be experiencing the joy that takes place when they are in each other's presence.

---

4. See *Sefer Hama'amarim* 5657, "*Samach Tisamach*."

KODESH AND MIKRA KODESH

We can further understand the spiritual difference between *Shabbat* and *Yom Tov* by noting that in Scripture, *Shabbat* is called *kodesh* (holy).[5] *Kodesh* refers to something intrinsically and independently holy.[6] In contrast, *Yom Tov* is called in Scripture and in the liturgy *mikrah kodesh*.[7] This is usually translated a holy convocation, but *mikra*, as explained by the *Zohar*,[8] is also related to *kara* (to invite). Thus, we invite holiness, implying that the day itself is an ordinary weekday by nature (most holidays fall on weekdays), but that we can invite holiness into it from its higher source.

The drawing down of holiness on *Yom Tov* is in marked contrast to *Shabbat*, when the distinctive spiritual theme of the day is the elevation of all physical and spiritual levels. On *Yom Tov* we bring holiness down, so to speak, allowing it to permeate the lower realms. Thus, the Talmud states that Shabbat is *mekadsha vekaima* (inherently holy),[9] while on *Yom Tov inhu dekadshinhu lizmanim*—they [the Jewish People] sanctify the times. The holidays are determined based on when the *Sanhedrin* declares the date of the new moon. Unlike *Shabbat*, then, the holiness of *Yom Tov* is dependent on the spiritual service of the Jewish people.[10]

The Torah refers derisively to "the dung of your festivals"[11] in reference to one who eats on a festival motivated by gluttony and

---

5. Exodus 31:14.

6. *Zohar* II 94b.

7. All the holidays are called *mikra kodesh* (See Numbers 28:18, 25; 29:1 etc.).

8. III:93b.

9. *Beitza* 17a.

10. *Torah Or* 69g.

11. Malachi 2:3.

who fails to invite the poor to his table since he shows no concern for the sanctity of the festival.[12] Interestingly, it makes no reference to "the dung of your Sabbaths" because the physical aspects of *Shabbat* exist on an elevated level.[13]

The *Yom Tov* meal is called "dung" if poor people are absent as guests because *kelipah* exists on *Yom Tov* since it is a week-day. Having guests prevents the *kelipot* from deriving nurture from holiness[14] at that meal as would occur if it was eaten in gluttony. Inviting the poor to share in the *Yom Tov* meal accomplishes *avodat habirurim*, the spiritual service of sifting through physicality and elevating the sparks of holiness. Since the food is used for the mitzvah of providing for the *Yom Tov* needs of the poor, it is thus sanctified in being used for a holy purpose. This also emphasizes that the emotion connected with the spiritual service of *Yom Tov* is joy in particular, since when one experiences joy, he wants everybody else to be joyful.[15]

CHACHMAH AND BINAH

Unlike *Shabbat*, when one is prohibited to do any of the thirty-nine prohibitions, on *Yom Tov* we are only forbidden to do work that is classified as *melachot avodah* (works of labor). Those activities that pertain to eating, such as cooking, baking, etc., are permissible. Since all aspects of a holiday derive from its spiritual source, obviously something spiritually different happens on *Yom Tov*.

---

12. *Shabbat* 151b.
13. *Likkutei Sichot*, vol. 2, p. 564.
14. "*Yenikat hachitzonim*" in kabbalistic terminology.
15. *Torah Or* 15d.

On both *Yom Tov* and Shabbat a lofty spiritual light shines. This is indicated in the case of *Yom Tov* by the name *Yom Tov* itself. On that day, a light shines that is called *Tov*, which is the same as the infinite light God created on the first day. This is the light created on the first day of creation, about which scripture states, "And God saw the light that it was good."[16] It was so powerful that it was more than the world could bear, and it had to be hidden until the time of the world-to-come. On *Yom Tov*, however, this light does shine.

Nevertheless, the very lofty spiritual light on *Yom Tov* is still from a lower level than that of *Shabbat*. The light of *Shabbat* derives from the spiritual level known as *chachmah* (wisdom) whereas *Yom Tov* derives from the level known as *binah* (understanding).[17] The light of *chachmah* that shines on *Shabbat* is related to the spiritual level of delight discussed above.[18]

These spiritual levels can be understood by considering the corresponding levels in a human being. In the development of an idea, *chachmah* is the initial flash of insight. As of yet it has undergone no intellectual development, and therefore there are no details or ramifications connected to it. Once it begins to be worked out with all of its implications and all the concepts involved in understanding it have been clarified, it has progressed to the stage of *binah*. At the stage of *chachmah*, an idea is purer than at the level of *binah* and it involves less of the person's selfhood. The reason is that understanding it always involves the person's faculties and intellectual traits, which give his under-

---

16. Genesis 1:4.

17. *Likkutei Torah, Tzav*, 11d.

18. In kabbalistic terms delight is the source of the inner dimension of *chachmah*.

standing a personal aspect. For this reason, *chachmah* is associated with humility and the absence of ego, corresponding to a key term in chasidic philosophy—*bitul*—self-nullification. *Bitul* is a sense of complete subservience to God, recognizing that God is the only true existence and that the person is essentially non-existent.[19] This is alluded to in the spelling of the word *chachmah*, which can be alternatively read as *koach mah*—the power of what.[20] The word *mah* (what) is associated with humility, as when Moses and Aaron said *Venachnu mah*? (What are we?)[21]—implying, "We are nothing." The distinction between the divine levels of *chachmah* and *binah* is similar. *Chachmah* represents a loftier and more refined light than the light of *binah*. Since *chachmah* is associated with *bitul*, it can express God's essence since it operates in the absence of a sense of self-existence, which would obstruct the expression of God's total unity.

We can now understand the permissibility of work connected to food preparation on *Yom Tov*. An extremely subtle evil remains in the world and therefore a certain amount of work is permitted in order to elevate it to holiness. This is another example of *avodas habirurim*, as discussed above. On *Shabbat* this impurity[22] vanishes because of the light that shines. Therefore, it is forbidden

---

19. This service of *bitul* is particularly associated with the *Shalosh Regalim*—the Three Pilgrimage Festivals. The term *Regalim* derives from the word *regel* (foot) and classic sources stress literally being able to go up to Jerusalem on foot for the festival. Spiritually, the foot represents the service of *bitul* because the foot unquestioningly obeys the commands of the brain without any need to understand the commands or to be motivated about them.

20. *Tanya*, ch. 18.

21. Exodus 16:7.

22. "*Kelipat nogah*" in mystical terminology.

to work on *Shabbat* since the purpose of working and dealing with the world is to elevate this impurity, and on *Shabbat* there is none in the first place.[23] Analogously, the stronger the light, the less the darkness. Impurity, which conceals Godliness, is likened to darkness in concealing what is true and is obvious, in this case the reality of God's transcendent unity. Impurity also resembles darkness in that there are different degrees of darkness. In the brighter light of *Shabbat* all spiritual impurity is dispelled.

The names *Yom Tov* and *Shabbat* emphasize the above point: *Yom Tov* is a day, (i.e., a special day), but nevertheless a day. The name *Shabbat* implies something far beyond a holy day, so its name does not contain the word "day" at all.

SOWING AND REAPING

We can explore another dimension of joy on Yom Tov by exploring the observation of *Rabbeinu* Bechaya[24] that the three pilgrimage festivals, *Pesach*, *Shavuot*, and Sukkot were established according to the different times of the grain crop during the year. *Pesach* is in the month of *Aviv* (standing grain.)[25] *Shavuot* is called *Chag Hakatzir*[26] (the Festival of Reaping [of wheat]), and Sukkot is called *Chag Ha'asif* (the Festival of the Harvest).

The reason that holidays of the year are established according to the time of the grain crop, as explained in chasidic philosophy, is that the Jewish people are called the "grain of God," as scrip-

---

23. *Torah Or* 15d.
24. Exodus 13:4, 23:17.
25. Exodus 13:4, see Rashbam.
26. Exodus 23:16.

ture states, "Israel is holy to God, the first of His grain."[27] This can be explained as meaning that the descent of the soul of a Jew to this Earth is like planting in the ground. As our Sages say, "Does not a man sow one *kor* in order to harvest many *korim*?"[28] The ultimate goal of the sowing is to have a large crop, that much grain should grow from a single kernel. It is the same way with the Jewish people: The ultimate goal of their "planting" in the earth, which is a very great descent, is the "sprouting" and growth of the soul afterwards, an ascent. Ultimately the soul reaches a much higher level than the one it occupied before coming down to this world.

Moreover, this comparison to grain also teaches the correct manner of a Jew's spiritual service.

1. The sprouting is not from the grain itself, but rather from its decay. The seed decays and becomes completely nullified to the divine power of growth that God created in the soil. This in turn elicits the power of growth to cause new plants to sprout. From this we can understand something else, that the increase in grain is not just an increase in quantity (that the result is much more than the input) but rather a whole new existence comes about.

2. It is the same way with the descent and subsequent ascent of the soul: The way to achieve the sprouting of the soul through planting in the earth is through an approach of *bitul* (corresponding to the decay of the seed). We have already discussed *bitul*—self-nullification—in this chapter as a quality of *chachmah*. In this context, *bitul* means the service of accepting the heavenly yoke, becoming completely

---

27. Jeremiah 2:3.
28. *Pesachim* 87b.

subservient to God's will. This is what Rabbi Schneur Zalman of Liadi calls the "beginning and foundation of all spiritual service."[29] When the soul achieves an ascent and "sprouts," its level then far surpasses its prior one. Like the new grain, it is as if it has achieved a veritable new existence.

3. In connection with physical planting, scripture states, "Those who sow with tears will reap with joyous song. [Though] he walk along weeping carrying the bag of seed, he will return with joyous song carrying his sheaves."[30] This verse stresses that by sowing with weeping and crying specifically (which is a state of *bitul* since the one weeping is in an abject state and feels himself to be lowly) one comes to "reap with joy . . . he will return with joyous song carrying his sheaves." It is the same way with the service of the Jewish people: Through *bitul* they come to the time of "sprouting" and the revelation of Godliness. They then rejoice in their closeness to God.

In spiritual service, the joy revealed at the time of the ascent is not an incidental matter (i.e., that since a Jew sees that there is "sprouting" he is happy). Rather, it is part of the ascent itself: It is specifically through joy that an ascent occurs that can be considered a new level of existence.

This accords with the above-stated principle that "joy bursts all boundaries"; true joy can nullify all a person's limits and limitations, and this is the wondrous ascent achieved in the soul through its spiritual labor in the world.

---

29. *Tanya*, beginning of ch. 41.
30. Psalms 126:5–6.

12

🙖

Rosh Chodesh:
Revealing the Spiritual
within Nature

"And on your day of gladness, and on your festivals, and on your new
moons . . ." (Numbers 10:10).

Rosh Chodesh, the first day of the lunar month, is called "the
head of the month" and not the "beginning of the month" for a
reason similar to the explanation for the name Rosh Hashanah:
Just as the head contains the life-force for all the limbs, and just
as the life-force of all the limbs remains connected to the head
even after it is drawn into all the limbs, *Rosh Chodesh* includes
the life-force for all the days of the month. Another implication
of the name *Rosh Chodesh* is that when a person performs his
spiritual service during the days of the month, he must draw upon
the spiritual arousal that occurred on *Rosh Chodesh*.[1] The sec-

---

1. *Sichat Shabbat Parshat Chayei Sarah* 5711, p. 82.

ond part of the name *Chodesh* is related to *chadash* (new). In simple terms, this refers to the renewal of the moon, the birth of the new moon. In kabbalistic sources, however, it is explained that every *Rosh Chodesh* brings a new spiritual light, one that never illuminated before throughout time.[2] This light derives from a completely new general revelation that takes place every Rosh Hashanah and that is divided up for the twelve months of the year. When each *Rosh Chodesh* arrives, its particular new light illuminates.

The association of newness with the word *Chodesh* has important implications for a person's spiritual service. The Jewish people are compared to the moon, and "reckon by the moon,"[3] and "are destined to be renewed like it."[4] Through the *chidush*, the new spiritual element that is accomplished in the world through the service of the Jewish people, the Jewish people achieve a new level higher than the one they occupied before coming down into the physical world. This will be finally revealed in the future redemption. One might say that each *Rosh Chodesh* there is revealed in each individual Jew the spark of *Mashiach* that is within him,[5]

---

2. The renewal of the moon itself has a kabbalistic dimension. The moon corresponds to the *sefirah* of *malchut* in that it "has no light of its own" and shines with reflected light from the sun. Similarly, the spiritual "light" of *malchut* is only what it receives from the *sefirot* above it. Just as the moon becomes smaller and smaller until it is not visible immediately before its rebirth, similarly *malchut* receives its light from the *sefirot* above it by "nullifying itself" in its yearning to receive this light. In the same way, the Jewish people (who are compared to the moon, etc.) are able to become a vessel for God's light through exhibiting the trait of "*bitul*" (self-nullification).

3. See *Sukkah* 29a.

4. Liturgy, *Kiddush Lavanah*; *Sanhedrin* 42a.

5. See *Ma'or Einayim*, end *Parshat Pinchas*.

the level of *yechidah*,[6] which is a spark from the level of general *yechidah*, the soul of *Mashiach*. This revelation accomplishes a *chidush* in the person's whole existence and everything that pertains to him: The level of *yechidah* permeates him.[7]

The spiritual character of *Rosh Chodesh* can best be explained by contrasting it with *Shabbat*. Each of these two days expresses one mode of a basic two-fold pattern in spiritual service, a pattern that is also built into the structure of creation: elevation and drawing down. *Rosh Chodesh*, on which work is permitted, represents drawing down the spiritual into the earthly and mundane. *Shabbat*, on which work is forbidden, represents elevation, as the mundane and the earthly become more spiritual. This two-fold pattern is also illustrated at the giving of the Torah, for instance, when we are told the God descended onto the mountain and also that Moses went up. The two modes of this pattern also have a reciprocal relation: An elevation brings a corresponding drawing down, and a drawing down brings a corresponding elevation. The *Shabbat* elevation of the physical world and all the levels of the spiritual realm is followed by the drawing down of spiritual delight. The drawing down of a higher level of Godliness on *Rosh Chodesh* brings an elevation to the life-force creating the world.

Although *Rosh Chodesh* is unlike *Shabbat* and *Yom Tov* in that work is permitted, we read in the Torah, "Thus says God, the gate of the inner court that faces toward the east shall remain closed on the six working days, but on *Shabbat* it shall be opened, and on *Rosh Chodesh* it shall be opened,"[8] indicating that *Rosh Chodesh* is not considered a regular work day and retains a separate iden-

---

6. See chapter on Yom Kippur.
7. *Sichat Parshat Toldot* and *Rosh Chodesh Kislev* 5752.
8. Ezekiel 46:1.

tity. Similarly, the Torah says elsewhere, "Tomorrow is *Rosh Chodesh . . .* you shall come to the place where you hid on the day of work."[9] It is actually on a higher level than an ordinary weekday, which is why an additional sacrifice was brought in the days of the Temple called the *karban musaf,* to which the *Musaf Amidah* prayer that we say now corresponds. This is also the reason we say the prayer of *Hallel.*

We can understand the unique status of *Rosh Chodesh* further by noting that the Torah says about work on a weekday "six days you shall work,"[10] using language that implies a command to work. Even though the evident simple meaning is that work is merely permitted on the six weekdays, the *Midrash Mechilta*[11] states that there is, in a sense, an obligation to work.

Chasidic philosophy explains that by doing work following the guidelines of the Torah (doing business honestly, etc.), one brings about the meaning of the statement "in six days God made the Heavens and the Earth,"[12] the elicitation of a divine light to create and give life to the world, a divine light clothed in nature. We must elicit this from God, because for Him this is descent.

On *Shabbat,* by contrast, it is forbidden to do work, for spiritually *Shabbat* is higher than the level of "in six days God created, etc." Then a divine light shines that is not clothed in nature. By violating the prohibition of work on *Shabbat,* we cause God to contract Himself, as explained in the chapter on *Shabbat.*[13]

---

9. I Samuel 20:19.

10. Exodus 20:9.

11. Exodus 20:9.

12. Exodus 20:11.

13. In kabbalistic terms this means causing a descent of *malchut* into *middot,* corresponding to the work of sifting and purifying, and contrary to the spiritual character of *Shabbat,* when *malchut* ascends to *chachmah.* (*Torat Shmuel* 5630).

In contrast, on *Rosh Chodesh* nature itself is on a higher level. In other words, *Shabbat* represents a mode that is higher than nature, a weekday represents a mode that accords with nature, and *Rosh Chodesh* elicits that which is higher than nature and allows it to permeate nature.[14]

These different levels are based on the various divine attributes through which God creates the world. Chasidic philosophy explains that on *Rosh Chodesh* the world is being created through God's speech (the ten "utterances," "Let there be light," etc.) just as on the rest of the days of the month. However, this method of speech, in Kabbalistic terms, is the attribute of *malchut* (kingship). *Malchut* in general is compared to the moon, which doesn't have its own light, but rather reflects the light of the sun. In the same way, *malchut* is a reflection of the other nine attributes. Throughout the month, the higher three of the ten attributes, the intellectual ones—wisdom, understanding, and knowledge—have to be condensed and be expressed with the emotional attributes acting as intermediaries. Only then is the energy of these higher levels received by *malchut*.

This can be understood by way of analogy by considering a person. Normally a person's power of speech and power of action relate to his intellect with the emotions acting as an intermediary. The intellect itself is mainly concerned with the person himself understanding something. He speaks about something or engages in an action connected to it because he loves it.[15] Even concerning such typically intellectual matters as astronomy or medicine he normally speaks because he feels a certain interest or excitement about the matter he speaks about it.

---

14. Last five paragraphs *Torat Menachem* 5711, vol. 1, pp. 83–84.
15. *Likkutei Torah, Devarim,* p. 194 (daf 97c).

However, occasionally the speech and deed proceed directly from the intellect (not through the emotions)[16] as when there is an intellectually compelled necessity to speak or act based on one's understanding.[17] Therefore, though on *Rosh Chodesh* it is permitted to do work, nevertheless it is not considered a weekday, since action and speech (associated with *malchut*) on *Rosh Chodesh* proceed directly from wisdom (intellect), not by way of the emotions.[18]

The direct progression of wisdom to speech represents total self-nullification since wisdom, being an initial flash of insight, is intrinsically humble. At the stage of *chachmah* the person's own intellect and personality has not yet become involved with working out the concept, which happens at the stage known as *binah*. The absence of emotions as an intermediate stage means that wisdom retains this quality because the intermediate stages involve an idea acquiring dimensions and a personal significance. The corresponding elevation that follows the drawing down of wisdom into speech occurs when the person conducts himself in

---

16. When the light of intellect goes directly to speech, then it is totally characterized by the quality of *bitul*, self-nullification, since emotions represent the self while wisdom has the characteristic of *bitul*, as it says, "The words of the wise spoken quietly are heard" (Ecclesiastes 9:17)—*Derech Mitzvotecha*, p. 138.

17. This bypassing of the emotions by intellect is what is meant by *sha'ar hechatzeir haponeh kadim* (the gate of the inner court that faces toward the east). *Poneh* (facing) connotes facing directly, without intermediates. *Kadim* (east) is associated with wisdom, and *kadim* is related to *kodem* (prior or initial) also suggesting wisdom, since wisdom is the initial revelation of Godliness, the beginning of the sequence of *sefirot*.

18. Last two paragraphs of *Sefer Hama'amarim* 5744 (unedited), pp. 2053–2054.

accordance with the revelation of Godliness of the holiday, becoming closer to God in the process.

As mentioned previously, pure intellect is objective and not bound by outcomes or emotions. Once intellect actually brings one to feel in a certain way, that level of intellect is no longer pure, but condensed and limited. Therefore, when *malchut* receives its light of intellect through the emotions, it is not at all the same as when *malchut* receives its light directly from the forces of intellect.

On *Shabbat* the world exists directly from God's thoughts. The level of thought is not hidden in the garments of nature. This is why we are not allowed to work on *Shabbat*, since by working we cause a descent in the world so that Godliness is expressed through speech, which is a condensed light that is clothed in nature.

On *Rosh Chodesh*, nature is created by a higher form of God's speech so that nature itself takes on a higher form.

This is why we say *Hallel* on *Rosh Chodesh*, but not during the week or on *Shabbat*. The verses of *Hallel* speak of how God conducts Himself through miracles. During the week God wants us to conduct ourselves according to nature, making a vessel, a natural way for God's blessings to be manifested. We are not allowed to rely on miracles and therefore the Talmud compares saying *Hallel* on a weekday to "cursing and blaspheming."[19]

On *Shabbat* we don't say *Hallel* since we are not allowed to work. *Shabbat* is a result of preparation (i.e., the work is already completed), as indicated by the saying that "one who works before *Shabbat* is able to eat on *Shabbat*."[20] However, *Rosh Chodesh*

---

19. *Shabbat* 118b.
20. *Avodah Zarah* 3a.

is an intermediate between *Shabbat* and weekdays. We say *Hallel* to ask God to allow our work and weekday concerns to be permeated with the spiritual, a uniting of the physical and the spiritual, which is associated with miracles.

On *Rosh Chodesh* the saying of *Hallel* is a custom, unlike the recitation of *Hallel* on *Chanukah* and *Yom Tov*, when it is a law. The reason is that on *Rosh Chodesh* the miraculous permeates the natural and weekday activities so that the weekday activities are revealed and the miraculous is hidden. This is in contrast to *Yom Tov* and *Chanukah*,[21] which are associated with visible miracles, the military victory of the few over the many on *Chanukah* for instance.

Chasidic philosophy explains that *Rosh Chodesh* and *Shabbat* each have an advantage over the other. The advantage of *Shabbat* is that it is spiritually loftier than any weekday, and therefore it is forbidden to work. On the other hand, that in itself is the advantage of *Rosh Chodesh* over *Shabbat*: It is permitted to work and the elicitation of Godliness reaches farther, "all the way down" into the workday world. This gives it an advantage in achieving the goal of a "dwelling here below." On *Shabbat* time and space themselves are elevated, as if *Shabbat* is a different world, but the ultimate objective is to draw down Godliness into this world.

This concept is identical to the advantage of *Purim* over the rest of the holidays.[22] Even though from one perspective there is something lacking in a miracle clothed in nature (and there᠎e

---

21. *Sichat Parshat Chayei Sarah* 5711, p. 84.

22. The reason we do not say *Hallel* on *Purim* is that "we are still slaves of Achashverosh." This means that the miracle of *Purim* is clothed in nature and we needed to present requests to Achashverosh and seek to influence him in order to nullify the decree against the Jews, and afterwards we remained "slaves to Achashverosh."

we do not say *Hallel*), from another perspective there is an advantage to this kind of miracle: Since it is clothed in nature it shows the greatness of the divine light in even being able to permeate nature itself, and therefore the joy of *Purim* is greater than on any other holiday.[23]

The differences we have been talking about between *Shabbat* and *Rosh Chodesh* apply to these two days as they exist now. However, in the future, when *Mashiach* comes, the Torah states "Then all flesh will come to bow down before Me every *Rosh Chodesh* and *Shabbat*"[24] This means that the pilgrammage up to the holy Temple associated with the holidays in the days of the Temple will take place every *Shabbat* and *Rosh Chodesh*.[25] The spiritual revelation of *Shabbat* and *Rosh Chodesh* will have reached a new and higher level.

---

23. *Sichat Shabbat Parshat Chayei Sarah* 5711.

24. *Isaiah* 66:23.

25. *Sefer Hama'amarim* 5744 (unedited), p. 2054.

Index

ABOUT THE AUTHOR

Noson Gurary is an ordained rabbi and Jewish judge. He received his rabbinical ordination at the United Lubavitcher Yeshiva in Brooklyn, New York and his doctorate in Jewish philosophy from Moscow Lomonosov University in Russia. He is currently the executive director of the Chabad Houses in upstate New York and has taught in the Judaic Studies Department at State University of New York, Buffalo, for the past thirty years. Rabbi Gurary is the author of numerous articles published in rabbinical publications as well as *The Thirteen Principles of Faith: A Chasidic Viewpoint* (Jason Aronson Inc., 1996) and *Chasidism: Its Development, Theology, and Practice* (Jason Aronson Inc., 1997). He is a descendent of great chasidic masters, including Maggid of Mezhirech, Rabbi Levi Yitzhak of Czernobyl, and Rabbi Yisroel Ruzhin. Rabbi Gurary lives in Buffalo, New York with his wife and seven children.